gluten-free

Favorite Homestyle Recipes and Cooking Tips

susan bell

This cookbook is dedicated to my mother, Carol George, and sisters, Mary Beth Wright and Cyndi Wakefield, who have contributed delicious recipes and have helped immensely with this cookbook. Additionally, I will always be grateful to my husband, who has expanded my vision toward a greater summit.

Published by CreateSpace.com

Printed in the United States of America

Cover design by Carolyn Cahoon
Typography by Brian Talbot

The publisher and author are not responsible for health concerns that require medical supervision. Every effort is made to provide the latest information on gluten-free products included in the recipes.

Labels on products must be read to ensure that gluten has not been added since the publication of this cookbook. The author assumes no responsi-bility for errors or changes that occur after publication.

Foreword

by Dr. Peter H.R. Green of the Celiac Disease Center at Columbia University
and author of Celiac Disease: A Hidden Epidemic

People with celiac disease, and gluten sensitivity, need to own a copy of Susan's book. It is a great resource presented in a beautiful way. The recipes add diversity and nutrition to a diet that frequently lacks these important components.

Celiac disease is common, occurring in about 1% of the population world-wide. It is unfortunate that the majority are as yet undiagnosed. This is mainly due to lack of physician awareness about the disease: neither its frequency, great variety of manifestations, nor its ease of diagnosis. As a result the bulk of those with the diagnosis are unaware how their life could be altered by adopting a gluten-free life style.

The major result of this massive under-diagnosis is that those with celiac disease suffer from inadequate support systems. There is insufficient food labeling, lack of awareness in the food industry, inadequate knowledge among chefs and a generally inadequate availability of gluten-free products. When available they are usually more expensive than their regular gluten containing counterpart. School, college and eating out of the home are a minefield. Susan's book helps fill the void. It is readily readable and the items taste great!

People with gluten sensitivity are characterized by the presence of symptoms that are relieved by avoiding gluten, found in wheat, rye and barley. These people are often self diagnosed and could in fact have celiac disease. To diagnose celiac disease one typically requires a small intestinal biopsy and documented improvement, both clinical and pathological improvement. Blood tests often suggest the diagnosis; a small intestinal biopsy confirms it. We encourage a biopsy because one needs to be certain of the diagnosis prior to a life-long commitment to a gluten-free diet. This especially applies to children.

We at the Celiac Disease Center at Columbia University are attempting to fill the medical void by increasing the quality of the patient care of those with celiac disease, educating health care professionals and facilitating a great variety of research projects. It is through dietician, nutritionist and physician education that more will be diagnosed with celiac disease and their care will improve. Until the numbers diagnosed with celiac disease increases the difficulties will continue. However, wonderful cookbooks like this one make the burden of the disease less.

Peter HR Green
Professor of Clinical Medicine
The Celiac Disease Center
Columbia University, New York

Introduction

by Amy Yoder Begley, Celiac Olympian

I started having stomach problems when I was eighteen and for ten years I was misdiagnosed. I was diagnosed with IBS, lactose intolerance, and anxiety. I also started having health problems. I developed a goiter and became hypothyroid. I was also anemic and amenorrheaic. I then developed stress fractures and found out I was osteopenic, even though I grew up drinking three glasses of milk a day. My symptoms got to the point where I was spending half the day in the bathroom. I could not eat within six hours of running or else I was in the bathroom every thirty minutes. I finally told the doctor that I could not live like this. After looking over my ten year medical history they decided I had Celiac Disease.

At first, I did not believe them. How could a wheat and gluten allergy cause all those symptoms? However, within three weeks, I was spending less time in the bathroom, I was not bloating after every meal and my stomach did not hurt as much. At first, it was hard and I ate a lot of chocolate. Then six months later I was able to tolerate milk again. At that point, I ate a lot of ice cream. I slowly started to find gluten-free alternatives. I missed a lot of foods but not the way they made me feel.

Now three years later I can see and feel the difference in my body. I am no longer anemic or amenorrheaic. Plus, I accomplished a life-long dream of making the Olympic Team in the 10,000 meters. I competed in Beijing representing the USA placing 26th. I would not have been able to accomplish this goal had I not gotten that Celiac Disease diagnosis. For some people the Celiac diagnosis is a prison sentence but for me I was set free. I no longer had pain or planned my day and training runs around bathroom locations. Giving up pasta, wheat, and gluten can seem like a huge sacrifice but the returns are worth it. I gave up wheat and gluten but in return I regained my health and the Olympic Dream.

Giving up wheat and gluten does not mean giving up your favorite foods. There are so many new gluten-free alternatives to try. There are also great people who have taken the time to turn old favorite recipes into gluten-free ones. This cook book is one of those places to start. Susan has taken some of the comfort foods and made them gluten-free. She has also filled the cook book with tips and advice on cooking and eating gluten-free. If you feel deprived of your favorite comfort meal, just open the pages and get started on gluten-free cooking.

Amy Yoder Begley, Celiac Olympian

Table of Contents

For many recipes in this cookbook, the serving sizes are for 6-8 people. Leftovers from most of the recipes can be refrigerated or frozen for later use, which saves time and effort.

Susan, Age 41

I remember having a lot of stomach discomfort when I was young. After I got married, I recall my husband noticing that almost every night after dinner, I was suffering from a stomach ache. I hadn't noticed that this was unusual, because it was so much a part of my life.

Several years ago, my sister told me celiac disease is genetic and since our mother has it, there was a chance that we could also have it. I was tested and diagnosed with celiac disease. Additionally, two of our children tested positively.

After my diagnosis, I remember feeling like I had gone into a period of mourning. Due to a change in my eating habits and the need to exclude wheat, barley, and rye from my diet, I had lost a part of my life that was happy and satisfying. In addition, for the first two years or so, we were unable to eat any dairy products either. I started to wonder if I could find anything to eat besides tortilla chips!

I began to look through my favorite recipes and decided that many could be altered and would still be workable with a gluten-free diet. I realized that I could still have a happy life. I knew that my attitude would make all of the difference in how our children handled their issues with the disease. Even though a gluten-free diet can be difficult at times, we have realized that our good health is worth it. We can do it!

Breakfast

Best Waffles

3 eggs, separated
1 ¾ c. milk, almond milk, or soy milk
½ c. canola oil
2 t. vanilla
2 T. melted butter
¾ c. brown rice flour
¼ c. sorghum flour
¼ c. potato starch
⅔ c. tapioca flour
⅛ c. corn flour
1 T. + 1 t. baking powder
2 T. sugar
½ t. salt

Heat waffle iron. (A Belgian waffle iron works very well for this recipe.) Separate the egg whites from the egg yolks, and place the egg whites in a tall measuring cup or glass bowl. Beat egg whites until stiff. Place egg yolks in a separate mixing bowl with milk, vanilla, melted butter, and oil and mix well. Add the dry ingredients and melted butter. Mix gently until combined. Fold in egg whites. Spray waffle iron with non-stick spray, if needed. Makes 11-12 waffles.

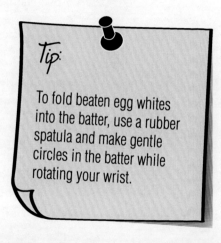

Tip:

To fold beaten egg whites into the batter, use a rubber spatula and make gentle circles in the batter while rotating your wrist.

Fluffy Oven Pancakes

⅓ c. butter
6 eggs
1 c. milk, almond milk, or soy milk
1 t. vanilla
¾ c. brown rice flour
¼ c. tapioca flour
½ t. salt

Preheat oven to 400 degrees. Melt butter in microwave. Pour butter evenly into 9" X 13" casserole dish. In large bowl, beat eggs, milk, and vanilla. Add rice flour, tapioca flour, and salt. Whip with hand mixer until well combined. Pour batter over melted butter. Bake for 22-24 minutes. Serve with powdered sugar and syrup. Makes 4-6 servings.

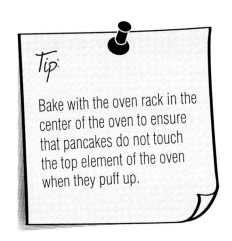

Tip:
Bake with the oven rack in the center of the oven to ensure that pancakes do not touch the top element of the oven when they puff up.

Favorite Pancakes

1 egg
½ c. applesauce
1 ½ c. milk, almond milk, or soy milk
½ c. oil
1 c. tapioca flour
⅓ c. sorghum flour
⅛ c. potato starch
⅛ c. corn flour
½ c. rice flour
1 T. + 1 t. baking powder
1 T. + 1 t. sugar
½ t. salt

Preheat griddle. Blend together the first four ingredients. Add dry ingredients. Stir until moistened. Fry pancake batter on non-stick griddle until pancakes are golden brown on each side. Makes 17-20 pancakes.

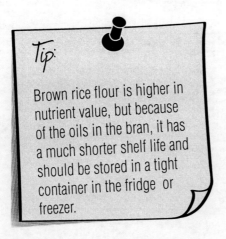

Tip:

Brown rice flour is higher in nutrient value, but because of the oils in the bran, it has a much shorter shelf life and should be stored in a tight container in the fridge or freezer.

Caramel Syrup

½ c. butter
½ c. milk
1 c. brown sugar
1 c. sugar
½ c. buttermilk
1 t. vanilla

Melt butter in a medium saucepan. Add milk, sugar, and brown sugar. Stir and boil gently for one minute. Remove pan from stove and add buttermilk and vanilla.

Delicious Dairy-Free Syrup

1 c. water
¾ c. sugar
1 c. brown sugar
1 c. corn syrup
⅛ t. salt
1 t. vanilla
½ t. butter flavoring

Bring ingredients to a boil in a medium saucepan and reduce heat to medium-high. Simmer for 1 minute.

Breakfast Burritos

1 T. butter
3 green onions, chopped
½ green pepper, chopped finely
1 t. crushed garlic
½ bag gluten-free hash browns, country style
2-3 eggs
Salt, pepper, garlic salt, to taste
1 c. grated cheese
Gluten-free corn tortillas
Salsa

Melt butter in skillet. Add green onions, green pepper, and crushed garlic. Sauté in melted butter for 2-3 minutes. Add hash browns and continue cooking until hash browns are warm and cooked through. Add eggs, salt, pepper, and garlic salt. Add cheese and heat until melted. Place a scoop of egg mixture in a warmed corn tortilla and top with salsa. Makes 5-7 servings.

Sausage Pizza

Crust:

2 T. butter
½ c. cornstarch
½ c. tapioca flour
¼ c. potato flour
1 t. sugar
½ t. salt
1 t. baking powder
1 egg
¾ c. milk

Preheat oven to 400 degrees. In a large bowl, blend butter and dry ingredients with pastry cutter (or mix in heavy duty kitchen mixer). In a small bowl, combine milk with the egg, and beat well. Pour milk and egg into mixture of dry ingredients and butter. Mix well. Place a clean sandwich bag on your hand and press dough onto one greased, large, round pizza pan. Bake 10 minutes. Remove from oven and add toppings.

Toppings for sausage pizza:

10 sausage links
2 T. brown rice flour
1 ½ c. milk
½ t. gluten-free chicken bouillon
4 eggs, with salt added
1 c. grated cheese

(Continued on next page)

Sausage Pizza, Cont'd.

Cook sausage* until browned and completely done. Remove sausage to a plate, leaving 2 T. fat and drippings in pan. Add rice flour and blend well with the drippings.

Stir in milk and chicken bouillon and bring to a boil. Cook gravy until thickened, stirring constantly. Spread gravy over the pizza crust. Cut sausage links into small chunks and spread on top. Scramble eggs and sprinkle over the pizza crust. Spread grated cheese over all.

Bake for 10-15 minutes. Best if allowed to set up for 5 to 10 minutes after baking. Makes 8-10 servings.

*To serve link sausage with a minimum amount of fat, place it in a frying pan and cover with a small amount of water (sausage may be pre-cooked in the microwave in a bowl). Cover pan and cook sausage slowly for 5 to 10 minutes. Drain well. With pan uncovered, continue to cook sausage slowly for 12 to 14 minutes until browned on all sides. Cover sausage with a small amount of water and cook for three minutes on high. Cook the sausage longer, if needed, to ensure the sausage is completely cooked.

Omelets

3 eggs
1 T. water or milk
3 mushrooms, sliced
¼ c. green peppers, diced
⅛ c. bacon pieces
⅛ c. green chilies
⅛ c. chopped olives
¼ c. green onions, diced
¼ c. cheese, grated

Whip eggs with water or milk. Pour into a greased omelet pan or non-stick frying pan. Sprinkle other ingredients on eggs. Follow instructions for omelet pan. If using a frying pan, place the toppings on one-half of the egg mixture and cook on medium heat until eggs turn light brown on the bottom. Then flip the uncovered half over onto the other half. Flip the entire omelet again to complete the cooking of the eggs. Makes 1 serving.

Tip:

If tender green peppers are desired, soften them by cooking them in a small amount of butter before starting the omelets.

Breakfast Pizza

Crust:

1 pkg. (24 oz.) hashbrowns, thawed
1 egg, beaten
½ t. salt
¼ t. pepper

Egg Topping:

7 eggs
½ c. milk
1 t. crushed garlic
½ t. salt
¼ t. pepper
1 c. chopped ham
¼ c. green onion slices
¼ c. chopped green bell pepper
1 ½ c. shredded cheese
Garlic salt, to taste
Salsa

Preheat oven to 400 degrees. Cover a large round pizza pan with cooking spray. Combine crust ingredients and spread across pizza pan, using the back of a spoon. Bake for 20 minutes.

For topping, whisk eggs, milk, garlic, salt, and pepper together. Spread over potato crust and top crust with remaining ingredients. Bake for 20-30 minutes, or until egg is fully cooked. Serve with salsa. Makes 8-10 servings.

Mexican Sausage Bake

4 white corn tortillas
1 cans chopped green chilies (optional)
½ lb. sausage, cooked and drained
1 c. Monterey Jack cheese
5 eggs
¼ c. milk
¼ t. salt
¼ t. garlic salt
¼ t. onion salt
¼ t. pepper
¼ t. ground cumin
Paprika
Sour Cream
Salsa

Preheat oven to 350 degrees. Beat eggs, milk, and seasonings. In a greased 8" X 8" baking dish, pour ⅓ of egg and milk mixture, and then layer half of the tortillas (slice them to fit in the square baking dish), chilies, sausage and cheese. Follow this layer with ⅓ of egg and milk mixture. Repeat layer of tortillas (slice them to fit in the square baking dish), chilies, sausage, and cheese. Cover with remaining ⅓ of egg and milk mixture. Sprinkle with paprika. Bake uncovered for 40-45 minutes. Let stand for 10 minutes. Serve with sour cream and salsa.

This dish can be prepared a few hours ahead or the day before, if covered and refrigerated. Remove from refrigerator 30 minutes before baking. Makes 4-5 servings.

Granola

7 brown rice cakes, in bite-sized pieces
½ c. slivered almonds
½ c. raw sunflower seeds
½ c. sweetened or unsweetened coconut
1 t. cinnamon
3 T. olive or canola oil
½ c. 100% pure maple syrup

Preheat oven to 300 degrees. Combine broken rice cakes, almonds, sunflower seeds, coconut, and cinnamon in a bag. Shake to distribute cinnamon evenly. Add oil and syrup. Shake bag until all is coated. Spray or grease cookie sheet. Bake granola 7 minutes, and stir. Bake an additional 8-10 minutes, or until granola is lightly browned.

Tip:

Place the rice cakes in a gallon-sized sealed bag and gently press with a rolling pin to break up into bite-sized pieces.

Fruit Smoothie

1 c. vanilla soy milk
1 c. ice cubes
1 c. sliced strawberries, raspberries, peaches, or mixed berries
¼ c. sugar
2 T. Nestle® Vanilla Nesquik®

Combine in blender using high speed until mixture is smooth. Makes 2-4 servings.

Orange Cream Smoothie

4 c. vanilla soy milk
½ can orange juice concentrate
½ c. sugar
¼ c. Nestle® Vanilla Nesquik®, or ¼ c. powdered milk, 2 T. sugar, and 1 t. vanilla
8 ice cubes

Combine in large blender using high speed for 1-2 minutes until mixture is smooth and sugar dissolves. Makes 8-10 servings.

Coconut Rice

2 c. short grain rice
¼ c. sugar
14 oz. coconut milk
Water
Additional sugar or brown sugar
Fresh or canned fruit

Soak rice in warm water for 20 minutes to soften. Preheat oven to 350 degrees. Pour coconut milk into a large measuring cup, add water to it to make 4 ½ c. liquid. Pour this liquid into a saucepan. Add sugar and simmer liquid until sugar dissolves.

Drain water off of rice. Pour drained rice and coconut milk/water mixture into a covered 9" X 13" casserole dish. Bake for 15 minutes, stir, and bake for 15-20 minutes more. If there is still a little liquid, it will gradually absorb into the rice. Serve rice with additional sugar or brown sugar (to taste) and fruit on top. Makes 6-8 servings.

*This recipe can also be used as a side dish. Omit the fruit and reduce the sugar.

Tip:

The use of soy milk or almond milk works well as a substitute in these recipes if you are intolerant to dairy products.

Tip;

Consider starting a support group for people in your area who have celiac disease. It may be very beneficial.

Rachelle, age 20

I started having headaches in the second grade. When the headaches started coming on a daily basis, my mom decided to take me to the doctor. It was the first visit of many visits to come. I had multiple blood tests, and went to the dentist, an allergist, a chiropractor, an ear nose and throat doctor, and other specialists. An optometrist had me do eye exercises, which helped some of my headaches, but not all of them.

I gained weight in 9th grade. Because I was physically active, there was no reason for me to gain weight. I started getting tired and anxious. I continued my doctor visits, but they were not able to provide an explanation for my symptoms. Then I went to college. One day on my way to class, I ate a cookie. I wasn't even to my class when my stomach started to hurt. I got through ten minutes of class before I had to leave.

The next semester I went to the doctor over a dozen times. I had a colonoscopy, and nothing really turned up. The only thing I could really have to eat or drink was hot chocolate, and that didn't ease my stomach pain either. It has been twelve years since my symptoms began, and I finally know the reason for my past pain. I am gluten and casein sensitive. Since I've been off gluten I have more energy than I've ever had. I'm more awake than I've ever been. I'm happier than I've ever been. Going off gluten is so much easier than I thought it would be. You can still eat cake and brownies, and they taste better than the brownies with gluten in them! It's so easy, and it makes your life so much better. You can do it! If I can do it, anyone can do it!

Breads and Muffins

Buttermilk Baking Powder Biscuits

1 c. mashed potatoes
2 T. butter

Prepare mashed potatoes from dried potatoes, according to package directions. (For some brands of dehydrated potatoes, making two serving sizes on package directions may equal one cup of mashed potatoes.) Add extra butter. The potatoes should be moist, creamy, and easily stirred, but not runny. Set aside.

Combine the following dry ingredients into a large mixing bowl:

¾ c. brown rice flour
¼ c. potato starch
1 c. tapioca flour
2 t. baking powder
½ t. baking soda
½ t. salt
½ t. xanthan gum

In a small mixing bowl, beat the following:

¾ c. buttermilk, soy, or almond milk
1 egg

Add the egg and buttermilk (or soy or almond milk) to the potato mixture and beat until smooth. (The use of buttermilk in bread recipes that call for milk will often give greater moisturizing qualities to the bread.) Add this mixture to the dry ingredients and mix lightly, but well.

(Continued on next page)

Buttermilk Baking Powder Biscuits, Cont'd.

Preheat oven to 400 degrees. Lay out a large piece of plastic wrap on the kitchen counter. Place ½ of dough on it and then cover with another large piece of plastic wrap. Roll out the dough that is placed between the plastic wrap with a rolling pin until the dough is smooth and almost 1" thick. Remove the top sheet of plastic wrap and cut biscuits with a biscuit cutter or a drinking glass. Place on a lightly greased cookie sheet. Repeat with the second half of dough. Bake for 13-15 minutes. When baking the biscuits, they will not brown a lot on the top, but it is important to lift one up and be sure that they are browned on the bottom. Makes 8-9 biscuits.

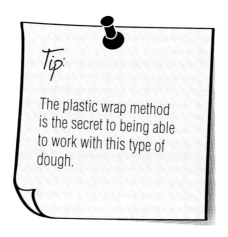

Tip:

The plastic wrap method is the secret to being able to work with this type of dough.

Banana Muffins/Bread

6 ripe bananas
1 c. canola oil
4 eggs
2 c. sugar
¼ c. corn flour
¾ c. sorghum flour
1 ½ c. tapioca flour
½ c. brown rice flour
¾ c. potato starch
1 T. xanthan gum
1 T. + 1 t. baking powder
½ t. salt

Preheat oven to 400 degrees. Use a blender to mix the bananas, oil, and eggs at high speed until smooth. Combine the dry ingredients in a mixing bowl. Add mixture in blender to dry ingredients and combine. (Overbeating the batter will cause the texture of the bread or muffins to become tough.)

Spoon batter into greased muffin tins, about ¾ full. Bake muffins for 20-25 minutes. This recipe freezes well. Makes 26-28 muffins.

For bread, use two greased pans (8 ½" x 4 ½" x 2 5/8") and bake the bread at 325 degrees for 45-55 min.

Zucchini Muffins/Bread

3 eggs, beaten
1 c. canola oil
2 c. sugar
1 T. vanilla
2 c. brown rice flour
1 c. tapioca flour
4 T. potato starch
1 t. salt
1 T. xanthan gum
¼ t. baking powder
1 t. baking soda
2 t. cinnamon
½ t. allspice
¼ t. nutmeg
1 ½ c. grated zucchini (either fresh or frozen)
½ c. water, if using fresh zucchini

Preheat oven to 400 degrees. Combine eggs, oil, sugar, and vanilla. Add dry ingredients and zucchini. Mix until combined. Spoon batter into greased muffin tins, about ¾ full. Bake muffins for 20-25 minutes. This recipe freezes well. Makes 24 muffins.

For bread, use two greased pans (8 ½" x 4 ½" x 2 5/8") and bake the bread at 325 degrees for 1 hour.

Poppy Seed Muffins/Bread

3 eggs
1 ⅛ c. canola oil
1 ½ c. milk or soy milk
1 ½ t. almond extract
1 ½ t. butter-flavored extract
1 ½ t. vanilla
2 c. sugar
2 c. brown rice flour
1 T. corn flour
2 ½ T. sorghum flour
1 ⅛ c. tapioca flour
⅓ c. potato starch, sifted
1 t. salt
1 ½ t. baking powder
1 t. xanthan gum
1 T. poppy seeds

Preheat oven to 400 degrees. Beat together the first six ingredients in a large mixing bowl. Add the dry ingredients and gently combine them into wet ingredients. After mixing, use a rubber spatula and press flat the largest remaining lumps in the batter. Spoon batter into greased muffin tins, about ¾ full. (Cupcake liners are helpful for these muffins, since they tend to stick to the muffin tins.) Bake for 20-25 minutes. If desired, poke holes in warm muffins or bread with a toothpick and pour glaze over them. This recipe freezes well. Makes 22-24 muffins or two loaves of bread.

For bread, divide batter into two greased 8 ½" x 4 ½" x 2 5/8" bread pans. Bake at 350 degrees for 1 hour or more.

(Continued on next page)

Poppy Seed Muffins/Bread, Cont'd.

Optional glaze:

¼ c. undiluted limeade or orange juice concentrate
1 c. powdered sugar
½ t. almond extract
½ t. butter-flavored extract
½ t. vanilla

Bring juice concentrate and powdered sugar to a boil for 1 minute. Remove from heat and add extracts and vanilla. Drizzle over muffins or bread.

Tip:

Since gluten-free breads have a tendency to fall apart, larger bread pans are not recommended.

Applesauce Muffins/Bread

2 eggs
1 ½ c. milk, almond milk, or soy milk
1 c. applesauce
1 c. canola oil
1 ¼ c. brown rice flour
½ c. sorghum flour
¼ c. corn flour
4 T. cornstarch or potato starch
1 c. tapioca flour
2 t. xanthan gum
1 c. brown sugar
½ c. white sugar
1 T. + 1 t. baking powder
1 t. salt
1 ½ t. cinnamon

Preheat oven to 400 degrees. Beat eggs. Add milk, applesauce, and oil. Add dry ingredients and mix just until moistened. Spoon batter into greased muffin tins, about ¾ full. Bake for 20-25 minutes. This recipe freezes well. For bread, divide batter into two greased 8 ½" x ½" x 2 5/8" bread pans. Bake at 350 degrees for 1 hour. Makes 24 muffins or two loaves of bread.

Pumpkin Muffins/Bread

8 eggs
1 ¾ c. oil
1 - 29 oz. can pumpkin
2 t. cinnamon
1 t. allspice
1 t. nutmeg
2 c. brown rice flour
1 ½ c. tapioca flour
½ c. sorghum flour
¼ c. corn flour
½ c. potato starch
4 c. sugar
1 T. + 1 t. xanthan gum
1 T. + 1 t. baking powder
1 T. + 1 t. baking soda
2 t. salt

This recipe is large enough for both bread and muffins. Mix first 6 ingredients well. Add remaining ingredients and mix only until combined.

Bread: Grease pans (8 ½" x 4 ½" x 2 5/8") and bake at 350 degrees for 60 min. Muffins: Spoon batter into greased muffin tins, about ¾ full. Bake for 26 minutes at 400 degrees. This recipe freezes well. Makes 24 muffins and 2 small loaves of bread.

Bread pans of the following sizes are recommended in gluten-free bread recipes (the dimensions are of the inside of the pan at the top edge of the pan):

8 ½ inch length x 4 ½ inch width x 2 5/8 inch depth
7 ¼ inch length x 3 5/8 inch width x 2 ¼ inch depth

Our Favorite Rolls

½ c. lukewarm water
2 t. yeast
2 t. sugar

¾ c. milk
½ c. buttermilk
(or 1 ¼ c. soy or almond milk)

2 c. brown rice flour
1 ½ c. tapioca flour
⅛ c. sugar
2 ½ t. xanthan gum
½ c. dried potato flakes
1 t. salt
½ c. canola oil or shortening
2 T. butter
2 eggs

Preheat oven to 170 degrees or warm setting.   Pour lukewarm water into a small bowl, and sprinkle yeast and sugar across the top of the water.   (To be sure the water is not too hot, put a couple of drops on the inside of your wrist and be sure that it is lukewarm.)

Microwave the milk and buttermilk for about 1 minute, or until hot. Combine flours, sugar, xanthan gum, potato flakes, and salt in large bowl. Using a heavy duty kitchen mixer is recommended.   Add yeast mixture, hot milk, oil, butter, and eggs into dry ingredients. Beat at high speed for 3 min. Spray muffin tins with cooking spray.

(Continued on next page)

Our Favorite Rolls, Cont'd.

Spoon dough into muffin tins, around ¾ full. Set muffin tray on open oven door to rise, with oven preheated to 150 degrees. Let rise for approximately 20 min. for rapid rise yeast and 30 min. for regular yeast. Place rolls in oven and turn heat up to 375 degrees. Bake for 20-24 minutes. Makes 16-18 rolls.

The rolls can be frozen if wrapped in Glad Press 'n' Seal® and placed in a sealed freezer bag to preserve moistness.

Serve with honey or jam. This roll also works very well for a lunch meat sandwich, with all of the toppings. (Check the label of the lunch meat for wheat, especially deli roast beef).

Breadsticks: See P. 153.

Cinnamon Rolls: Fill greased muffin tins about ½ full with roll dough. Sprinkle dough with cinnamon sugar. Add roll dough to fill the muffin tins to around ¾ full. Sprinkle roll dough with additional cinnamon sugar. Cover the rolls with Caramel Syrup (see P. 9) when serving.

Cream Cheese Rolls: Mix 8 oz. cream cheese with ¾ c. brown sugar, 1 ½ t. ground cinnamon, and 1 ½ t. ground nutmeg. Scoop mixture into a small plastic freezer bag. Cut a ½" opening diagonally on one corner of the bag. Fill greased muffin tins about ½ full with roll dough. Holding the bag upright, squeeze cream cheese mixture out evenly onto roll dough. Add roll dough to cover the cream cheese mixture and fill the muffin tins to around ¾ full. Top cooked rolls with a glaze made with a mixture of 1 T. melted butter, 1 c. powdered sugar, 2 T. water, ½ t. almond extract, and ½ t. butter extract.

Whole Grain Bread

1 c. brown rice flour
½ c. tapioca flour
¼ c. potato starch
½ c. quinoa flakes
1 c. teff flour
¼ c. sugar
½ t. salt
3 ½ t. xanthan gum
1 ½ T. yeast
1 ¾ c. warm water
¼ c. vegetable, canola, or olive oil
1 t. apple cider vinegar
½ c. reconstituted potatoes from dried potato flakes
3 eggs, beaten

Sift dry ingredients, if needed. Combine first 7 ingredients. Sprinkle yeast over the combined dry ingredients. Pour warm water over the top of the yeast and let it sit for 3 to 4 minutes. Add oil and vinegar and mix on low speed. Add water, etc., according to package directions, to make the potato flakes into ½ c. of mashed potatoes. Add beaten eggs and reconstituted potatoes. Beat on high speed for 3-5 minutes. Batter will be stiff. Spoon it into two small greased bread pans and pat dough with spoon to make each loaf smooth.

Preheat oven to 400 degrees. Let dough rise for about 20 minutes in a warm place, until it has risen 1 inch. Place in oven and turn the oven down to 350 degrees. Bake for approximately 30 to 35 minutes. Top will be browned, edges will be pulling away from the pan, and the top will be firm to touch. Bread will be very dense. *Quinoa is a complete protein with significant amounts of iron, potassium and magnesium. Teff is rich in iron, calcium, and fiber. Makes 2 loaves.

Quick Rice Bread

3 c. brown rice flour
1 ½ c. potato starch
2 c. tapioca flour
¾ c. sugar
2 T. xanthan gum
1 ½ T. baking powder
1 ½ t. salt
1 T. Nestle® Vanilla Nesquik® (optional)
3 c. milk or soy milk
6 eggs
¾ c. oil

Preheat oven to 375 degrees. Mix all dry ingredients first.
Add wet ingredients, beginning with milk. This recipe works
best with a heavy duty kitchen mixer. While it is mixing (for
about 45 seconds) on medium speed, spray or grease bread
pans. Turn off mixer and spoon soft dough into three small
8 ½" x 4 ½" x 2 5/8" loaf pans. Do not press dough down.
Bake at 375 degrees for 38-43 minutes. Bread will be puffed
up and not completely smooth on the top. It should be well-
browned on the sides and top, or otherwise the bread will be
condensed and sticky in the middle. Remove bread from bread
pans and place on wire rack. Allow to cool for 5-10 minutes
before covering bread with clean dish towels or paper towels.
Makes 3 loaves.

Use bread within one day or freeze it since rice bread goes
stale quickly. When bread has completely cooled, wrap slices
in Glad Press 'n' Seal® and place in a sealed freezer bag to
preserve moistness. The heavy duty plastic storage bag is re-
usable. This bread is great for French toast, cinnamon toast,
or served with butter and honey.

Butter-Topped Bread

1 ⅓ c. water
½ t. salt
⅔ c. butter
½ c. milk
1 ⅓ c. (or more) dried potato flakes

Bring the first four ingredients to a boil. Remove from heat and add dried potato flakes. The potatoes should be moist and creamy and easily stirred. Measure out 2 cups of the prepared potatoes. (Mashed potatoes help lessen crumbling and increase the moisture of the bread.)

2 c. lukewarm water
2 T. + 2 t. sugar
1 T. + 1 t. dry yeast granules

Pour water into a small bowl. Sprinkle yeast and sugar over the top of the water. Set aside. Preheat oven to 350 degrees.

4 eggs, well beaten
2 c. prepared mashed potatoes
4 c. brown or white rice flour
1 ⅓ c. potato starch
⅔ c. tapioca flour
½ c. dry milk powder
2 t. salt
1 T. + 2 t. xanthan gum
Yeast, water, and sugar mixture
3 T. butter (to spread onto top of each loaf)

(Continued on next page)

Butter-Topped Bread, Cont'd.

In a large mixing bowl, combine eggs and mashed potatoes. Add dry ingredients and yeast mixture and mix well.

(This recipe works well with an electric bread mixer.) Divide dough into three greased 8 ½" x 4 ½" x 2 5/8" bread pans (larger pans will not work as well). Cover your hand with a clean plastic bag and shape the dough into a loaf shape within the pan. Score the center of the top of the loaf from one end to the other (about ½ inch deep) and spread 1 T. butter/loaf lightly into the slit before baking. (In addition, brushing the top of each hot loaf of bread with butter will soften the crust and make it easier to cut.)

Let the bread rise for 30 minutes. Bake for approximately 40-45 minutes. The bread should be browned on the outside and firm to touch, but over-baking will decrease the moistness of the bread. Makes 3 small loaves.

*This bread is especially good when it is hot and may be frozen in individual slices for use when you want bread for French toast, or sandwiches, or to toast and serve with a creamed cheese sauce or chicken sauce. Place each slice in an individual sandwich bag and the bagged slices together in a heavy duty plastic storage bag. Place them in the freezer in a bread pan (for support to prevent breakage of slices).

Moist Corn Bread

1 c. butter
1 c. sugar
4 eggs
4 oz. can green chilies (optional)
1 16 oz. can creamed corn
½ c. shredded cheddar cheese (optional)
¾ c. rice flour
¼ c. tapioca flour
1 c. cornmeal
1 T. + 1 t. baking powder
½ t. salt

Preheat oven to 350 degrees. Cream the butter, sugar, and eggs. Add creamed corn and optional ingredients, if desired. Add dry ingredients. Pour into greased 9" X 13" baking dish. Bake for 35-40 minutes. Makes 12 servings.

Tip:

Earth Balance Spread® (a dairy-free margarine) is delicious and has been used successfully as a substitute for butter in the recipes in this cookbook.

Tip:

Xanthan gum is called for in most baked rice flour products. It helps the baked product to be more elastic and chewy and less dry and crumbly.

Tip:

Any bread items that include baking powder should be mixed only until combined.

Cyndi, age 56

I remember feeling sick after eating from the time I was a small child. I had a variety of health problems throughout my life. In the 90's, I had painful stomach problems which were diagnosed as gastritis and irritable bowel. I had a whole gamut of lab tests during this period of time, including the endoscopy and biopsy of the small intestine. There were some irregularities, but they were not recognized as damage from gluten. During this time, my daughter began to withdraw. She was having digestive problems that I was not aware of.

In 2000, I dropped rapidly in weight. For a while I was good with that, but then it got out of hand. Forty pounds later, I was emaciated. At that same time, my daughter started to swell when she ate. She sank into a severe clinical depression as well. By this time I had figured out that celiac disease might be her problem. She had blood tests that came back with high antibody and transglutiminase readings. That was a big red flag for me, but the doctor wouldn't diagnose Celiac Disease unless a small intestinal biopsy confirmed it. Her biopsy came back negative, although the doctor said there were some irregularities.

Two years later she was still eating gluten and still swelling and bloating when she ate. I was desperate to find a definitive diagnosis. Lucky for us, in 2003 I found a lab in Texas that would analyze some tests done in my own home. This included genetic testing. We discovered that my daughter had two gene markers for Celiac Disease and I had one. The tests also indicated that dairy was a problem for us as well. By that time, my health was so impaired that I couldn't walk without a walker. For both my daughter and me, it has been a long road back. Now I have reached a better weight. I am able to walk and exercise. My daughter has come out of her depression. She is able to hold a job, as well as take college classes.

Soups, Salads, and Sides

Clam Chowder

1 can minced clams
1 c. onion, finely chopped
1 c. celery, finely chopped
2 c. red potatoes, chopped
1 c. butter
¾ c. brown rice flour
4 c. milk or ½ and ½ cream (or 3 c. almond milk + 1 c. soy milk)
1 ½ t. salt
½ t. sugar
¼ t. pepper
1 t. gluten-free chicken bouillon powder
½ t. crushed garlic

Drain clam juice into water that barely covers the vegetables. Reserve clams until later. Simmer vegetables until tender. Do not drain. Make a white sauce by melting butter in a small saucepan and adding rice flour. Stir until combined and mixture begins to gently boil. Add milk (or cream or substitutes), salt, sugar, pepper, bouillon, and garlic. Stir over medium-high heat until thickened. Add cream sauce and clams to the vegetables and stir well. Makes 7-8 servings.

Tip:

Leave out clams and serve "potato soup" to the children who don't care for clams.

Curried Chicken Rice Soup

2 c. cooked chicken, cubed (can use canned chicken)
2 c. cooked long grain rice
2 large carrots, grated
2 celery stalks, finely diced
1 small onion, chopped
¾ c. butter or margarine
½ c. brown rice flour
⅛ c. corn flour
⅛ c. sorghum flour
1 t. gluten-free seasoned salt
1 t. curry powder
3 - 12 oz. cans of evaporated milk
4 c. chicken broth, or more

Cook chicken and rice. In large saucepan, sauté carrots, celery, and onions in butter until vegetables are tender. Add dry ingredients. Gradually add evaporated milk and chicken broth. Stir well. Add cooked chicken and rice. Simmer until soup is thickened to desired consistency. Add more chicken broth if soup is too thick. Makes 9-10 servings.

Minestrone Soup

3 slices bacon
½ t. crushed garlic
1 medium onion, diced
1 stalk celery, diced
2 carrots, finely diced or grated
1 potato, finely diced
8 c. chicken broth
28 oz. can diced tomatoes
15 oz. can kidney beans
1 t. dried basil leaves
2 t. dried parsley
½ t. salt
½ c. uncooked Tinkyada® Spaghetti Noodles
Garlic salt, to taste

Fry bacon in the large saucepan that the soup will be cooked in. Remove bacon and slice into small pieces. Sauté garlic, onion, celery, carrots, and potato in bacon grease for 25 minutes. Bring broth to a boil. Add vegetables, diced tomatoes, kidney beans, basil, parsley, and salt. Simmer soup for 45 minutes. Add uncooked noodles. (Break noodles into 2 inch pieces before measuring them.) Boil soup for 12-15 minutes, or until noodles are tender. Season the soup with garlic salt, to taste. Makes 8-9 servings.

Cream of Rice Soup

4 c. cooked rice
1 T. butter
1 lg. onion, chopped
3 carrots, grated
3 stalks celery, grated
½ c. butter
¾ c. rice flour
¼ c. sorghum flour
8 c. chicken broth
1 c. milk, soy milk, or almond milk
1 c. chopped, cooked ham
Pepper, to taste

Cook the rice. In a frying pan, melt 1 T. butter and sauté the vegetables in butter until tender. In a large pot, melt ½ c. butter and stir in rice and sorghum flour. Gradually add chicken broth, while stirring. Boil until thickened and add cooked vegetables, milk, cooked rice, cooked ham, and pepper. Makes 8-9 servings.

Sausage Vegetable Soup

1 lb. sausage
1 onion, chopped
1 bunch washed, chopped kale (avoid using the stem/spine)
7 c. low-sodium chicken broth*
4 unpeeled, diced potatoes
½ t. crushed garlic
½ t. oregano
Salt and pepper, to taste
1 can of evaporated milk, or 1 ⅔ c. almond or soy milk

Fry sausage and chopped onion until completely cooked. Drain grease. In a large pot, combine chicken broth, kale, potatoes, garlic, and seasonings. Bring to a boil. Add cooked sausage and onion. When potatoes are tender, add milk and serve. Makes 7-8 servings.

*If using water and chicken bouillon to make chicken broth, reduce the bouillon due to the salt level of the sausage.

Potato Bean Soup

5 c. gluten-free chicken broth
3 medium potatoes, finely diced
1 T. butter, melted
1 clove garlic, chopped (or ½ t. minced garlic)
½ c. celery, diced
2 medium carrots, shredded
½ onion, chopped
½ c. sour cream
1 T. brown rice flour
2 t. dried dill
⅛ t. pepper
15 oz. can great Northern white beans (not drained)

Add diced potatoes to boiling chicken broth. Turn heat down to medium high. Melt butter in frying pan. Stir fry the vegetables in butter and garlic until they are tender. Mix rice flour, dill, and pepper into sour cream. Remove chicken broth and potatoes from heat when potatoes are tender. Add sour cream, rice flour, and pepper mixture to chicken broth. Whisk soup until sour cream lumps disappear. Add white beans. Makes 4-5 servings.

Cream of Broccoli Soup

2 c. fresh or frozen broccoli, chopped
2 T. canola oil
½ onion, chopped, or 2 T. minced, dried onion
2 c. chopped celery
2 cloves garlic, minced
¼ c. butter
½ c. rice flour
4 c. milk, ½ and ½ cream, or almond milk
¼ t. marjoram
2 c. chicken broth
1 t. garlic salt

Steam broccoli until tender. In frying pan, sauté onions, celery, and garlic in canola oil until light brown and very tender. In large saucepan, melt butter. Add rice flour and stir well. Add milk and marjoram and bring to a gentle boil. Stir mixture with a whisk until it thickens. Add cooked vegetables and chicken broth. Sprinkle soup with garlic salt, and add more if needed. Makes 5-6 servings.

Chicken/Turkey Noodle Soup

2 turkey thighs (or 4 chicken thighs)
Water
2 stalks celery, chopped
¼ c. celery leaves
1 onion, chopped
¼ t. garlic powder
¼ t. minced garlic
Garlic salt to taste
2 c. gluten-free spaghetti noodles (break into small pieces and measure before cooking)

In a large saucepan, cover turkey with water. Boil turkey gently with celery, celery leaves, onion, garlic, and additional water, as needed. Boil gently for 3 hours, or until fully cooked. Remove turkey and de-bone. Boil noodles in broth and vegetables for around 15 minutes, or until tender. Add meat to the soup and bring to a boil for one minute. Makes 5-7 servings.

Baked Potato Soup

4 large baked potatoes, cooled
⅔ c. butter
⅔ c. rice flour
6 c. milk
¾ t. salt
½ t. pepper
4 green onions, chopped
12 slices bacon, cooked and crumbled
1 ¼ c. shredded cheese
8 oz. sour cream

Peel and cube baked potatoes and set aside. Discard the skins. Melt butter, add rice flour, and stir until smooth. Cook 1 minute stirring constantly. Gradually add milk and cook over medium heat, stirring constantly, until mixture is thickened and bubbly. Add potato cubes, salt and pepper, half of the green onions, half of the bacon, and 1 cup of cheese. Cook until thoroughly heated. Remove from heat and stir in sour cream. Add more milk if soup is too thick. Serve with remaining bacon, green onions, and cheese to sprinkle on top. Makes 6-8 servings.

Tip:

Most sour cream does not contain gluten. Occasionally, fat free sour cream can contain gluten. Please check the label.

Enchilada Soup

1 medium chicken breast or ½ pound ground beef
1 can chicken broth
1 can corn, with the juice
10 oz. can gluten-free green enchilada sauce*
1 can black beans, drained
Tortilla chips
Grated cheese
Sour cream

Cook and shred chicken or fry the ground beef. (Raw chicken can be added to the chicken broth and cooked before adding other ingredients, or the chicken can be baked or fried.) Combine chicken broth, corn, green enchilada sauce, and black beans. Add meat and simmer for 10 minutes. Serve with tortilla chips, grated cheese, and sour cream. Makes 4-5 servings.

*Depending on the brand of green enchilada sauce, this soup can be spicy.

Chicken Taco Soup

1 - 1 ½ c. potatoes, diced
2 c. raw chicken, cubed
4 c. water
2 t. gluten-free chicken bouillon
½ t. crushed garlic
1 can black beans
14.5 oz. can stewed or diced tomatoes
1 c. salsa
1 t. lemon juice
1 can corn (optional)
Grated Cheese
Sour Cream
Tortilla chips
Salsa

In a large saucepan, combine first five ingredients. Boil gently until potatoes are tender and chicken is fully cooked. Add black beans, stewed tomatoes, salsa, lemon juice, and corn (optional). Simmer for 10-20 minutes. Serve with grated cheese, sour cream, tortilla chips, and salsa. Makes 5-6 servings.

Fiesta Soup

2 turkey drumsticks
½ c. grated carrots
1 c. grated zucchini
1 can green beans, drained
¼ t. dried basil leaves
1 t. garlic salt
½ t. salt
1 t. pepper
1 ½ c. gluten-free spaghetti noodles (break into small pieces and measure before cooking)

Cover drumsticks with water in a large saucepan. Boil gently until done, about 2 - 2 ½ hours, or until completely cooked. Take meat off bones and cut into small pieces. Set aside. Pour strained broth back into the pot. Add water and chicken bouillon, if needed, to equal 2 quarts of broth. Add carrots, zucchini, green beans, basil, garlic salt, salt, and pepper. Bring to a boil. Cover and reduce heat to medium. Cook 15 minutes. Add gluten-free noodles and cook soup until noodles are tender. (Or cook the noodles in a separate pot while vegetables are cooking, and add cooked, drained noodles to the soup.) Add cooked turkey and mix well. Makes 6-7 servings.

Beef Taco Soup

1 lb. ground beef
1 onion, chopped
1 can corn (don't drain)
1 can kidney beans (drain and rinse)
2 cans diced tomatoes, 14.5 oz. each
1 c. water
1 pkg. gluten-free taco seasoning mix (or use the following and adjust according to taste: 1 T. chili powder, ½ t. garlic powder, 1 t. onion powder, ½ t. cumin, salt and pepper)
Tortilla chips
Shredded cheese

Brown ground beef with onion until cooked. Combine with remaining ingredients in a large saucepan. Simmer for 10-20 minutes. Serve with tortilla chips and shredded cheese. Makes 6-7 servings.

Thai Noodle Soup

2 boneless, skinless chicken breasts
4 pkgs. Thai Kitchen® Instant Noodle Soup-Spring Onion
6 c. water
5 t. gluten-free chicken bouillon powder
¼ t. ground ginger
¼ t. minced, fresh garlic
Cilantro, chopped
Green onions, sliced

Bake chicken breasts for 45 minutes at 350 degrees or boil in water for 50-60 minutes. Dice chicken. Prepare Thai noodles according to package directions, and add 2 cups of extra water to equal 6 cups. Add cooked chicken, ginger, and garlic. Top soup in bowls with chopped cilantro and green onions, if desired. Makes 4-5 servings.

Potato Cheese Soup

3 ½ c. water
2 c. diced potatoes
½ c. diced carrots
½ c. diced celery
¼ c. finely diced onion
½ t. salt

Combine all of the above ingredients in large saucepan. Boil gently until vegetables are tender. Drain vegetables, but reserve 1 c. of vegetable water.

½ c. butter
¼ c. brown rice flour
2 c. milk
¼-½ t. salt
¼ t. pepper
2 c. grated cheddar cheese

Melt butter in large saucepan. Add rice flour and stir well. Add milk, salt, and pepper, and cook over medium high heat until mixture thickens, stirring often. Add cheese and cooked vegetables. Add ½ c. of water saved from cooking vegetables and stir well. Continue adding water, ¼ c. at a time, until desired consistency is reached. Makes 3-4 servings.

Turkey Burger Soup

1 lb. turkey burger or ground beef
4 large potatoes, diced
1 carrot, grated
1 can green beans, drained
2 - 5.5 oz. cans of tomato juice (or 1 - 11.5 oz. can)
1 t. gluten-free beef bouillon
Garlic salt, to taste

Brown turkey burger in a frying pan until completely cooked. Peel and dice potatoes and place them in a large saucepan. Cover the potatoes with water. Grate carrots into the pan and boil both potatoes and carrots until tender. Add browned turkey burger, green beans, tomato juice, and bouillon. Add more beef bouillon for flavor, if needed. Sprinkle with garlic salt. Simmer until heated through. Makes 6-7 servings.

Mix for Easy Cream Soup

2 c. powdered non-fat dry milk
¾ c. cornstarch
¼ c. instant chicken bouillon (check label)
2 T. dried onion flakes
1 t. basil leaves
1 t. thyme
(2 t. Italian seasoning can be used in place of basil and thyme.)

Combine ingredients in a plastic bag and mix well. Store the soup mix in an airtight container until ready to use. Yield: Mix combined with liquid equals 9 cans of cream soup.

To substitute for 1 can of cream soup:

1. Combine ⅓ cup of powdered mix above with 1 ¼ cup cold water in small saucepan.
2. Cook and stir on stove top or in microwave until thickened. Allow mixture to cool before adding to recipe.
3. Add thickened mixture to casseroles as you would a can of soup. You can add mushrooms, chicken, etc., if desired.

Tip:

Make this ahead to allow time to thicken before using in a recipe.

Superb Ranch Dressing

Large Amount:

4 c. gluten-free mayonnaise
¾ c. buttermilk
1 ¼ c. milk
1 T. + 1 t. parsley
1 T. + 1 t. onion powder
½ t. garlic powder
1 ½ t. salt
1 t. pepper

Small Amount:

2 c. gluten-free mayonnaise
½ c. buttermilk or less
⅔ c. milk
2 t. parsley
2 t. onion powder
¼ t. garlic powder
¾ t. salt
½ t. pepper

Combine ingredients and stir with whisk until smooth. This dressing will stay fresh for several weeks. Stir well before serving.

Spinach Salad

4 c. iceberg lettuce
4 c. spinach
½ c. sliced almonds
3 T. sugar
½ T. butter
¼ c. green onions, chopped (or thinly sliced red onion)
½ c. mushrooms, sliced
2 T. grated Parmesan or Swiss cheese
2 T. bacon pieces
1 can Mandarin oranges

Tear lettuce and spinach into small pieces. Sauté sliced almonds in sugar and butter until sugar dissolves and almonds turn light brown. Combine lettuce and spinach with almonds and remaining salad ingredients. Serve with poppy seed dressing. Makes 7-8 servings.

Poppy Seed Dressing:

⅓ c. apple cider vinegar
2 t. poppy seeds
½ t. salt
½ c. sugar
½ t. onion powder
½ T. mustard
1 c. olive or canola oil

Blend first six ingredients until sugar is dissolved, then add oil. Mix well. This dressing is also excellent with steamed vegetables, including broccoli, cauliflower, carrots, or spinach.

Pear Romaine Salad

1 ½ t. apple cider vinegar
1 T. olive oil
½ t. sugar
1 ½ cups romaine salad mix
1 pear, cut-up
¼ c. cashews

Combine vinegar and oil. Toss with salad mix, pear, and cashews. Makes 1 serving.

Greek Salad

3 c. romaine lettuce, torn
1 cucumber, diced
1 tomato, chopped
½ c. sliced red onion
¼ c. feta cheese

Tear lettuce and cut up vegetables. Combine lettuce and vegetables and top salad with feta cheese. Makes 3-4 servings.

Dressing:

2 T. olive oil
2 T. fresh lemon juice
1 t. dried oregano leaves
½ t. salt

Blend until salt is dissolved. Pour over salad.

Chicken Cabbage Salad

1 c. cooked, cubed chicken
½ head of cabbage, sliced (or ½ bag coleslaw mix)
3 green onions, sliced
1 T. butter
¼ c. slivered almonds
2 T. sugar

Cook and cube chicken. Allow to cool. Place cabbage in salad bowl with green onions. Melt butter in small frying pan. Add sugar and almonds. Fry until almonds turn light golden brown. Cool slightly, then add carmelized almonds and cooked chicken to cabbage and green onions and mix well. Makes 4-6 servings.

Dressing:

⅛ c. honey
1 ½ T. canola oil
1 T. mayonnaise
1 T. gluten-free soy sauce
½ T. apple cider vinegar
½ t. salt

Blend dressing ingredients and pour them over combined salad ingredients.

Broccoli Salad

1 large bunch of broccoli, diced
½ c. raisins
⅛ c. bacon pieces
½ c. sunflower seeds
⅛ c. red onions, diced
½ c. mushrooms
1 c. mayonnaise
½ c. sugar
3 T. milk or soy milk
½ T. apple cider vinegar

Chop broccoli into small pieces. Add raisins, bacon pieces, sunflower seeds, red onions, and mushrooms. Make a salad dressing by mixing the remaining ingredients together. Add to broccoli mixture. Makes 6-8 servings.

Taco Salad

1 lb. ground beef
1 T. gluten-free taco seasoning mix (or 1 t. Mexican Seasoning)
2 c. gluten-free corn chips
4 c. chopped lettuce or salad mix
1 large tomato, chopped
1 c. grated cheese
½ c. black beans or gluten-free chili (optional)
Ranch dressing
Salsa

Cook the ground beef and drain the fat. Season the ground beef with seasoning mix. Cool slightly. Warm the beans or chili. Cool slightly. Combine all ingredients. Serve with ranch dressing and salsa. Makes 4-5 servings.

Tip:

If a substitute for cheese is needed, non-dairy Tofutti® American Cheese Slices may be cut into strips and added to salad. The company sells other great products as well.

Grilled Chicken and Vegetable Salad

1 lb. grilled (or fried) chicken or shrimp, diced
2 green bell peppers, diced
6 stalks of asparagus, cut into small pieces
4 c. Romaine and iceberg lettuce
1 medium tomato, diced
1 avocado, diced

Prepare dressing recipe below before starting salad ingredients. Grill or fry chicken or shrimp. Sauté the peppers and asparagus in cooking oil until tender. Toss vegetables with lettuce leaves, tomato, and avocado. Add chicken or shrimp. Pour dressing over salad when serving. Makes 5-6 servings.

Dressing:

½ c. olive oil
¼ c. fresh lemon juice
½ t. sugar
1 ½ t. dried basil
¼ t. salt
⅛ t. pepper

Combine and refrigerate for at least ½ hour before serving salad.

Corn Chip Salad

1 can kidney beans, drained
1 green pepper, diced
3 green onions, with tops, chopped finely
2 tomatoes, diced
1 small bag of Fritos® or other gluten-free corn chips
Kraft® Catalina Salad Dressing

Combine first 5 items. Just before serving add dressing and toss until well-coated. Makes 5-7 servings.

Tasty Mexican Salad

Sweet Pork

2 ½ lbs. pork (roast or country spare ribs)
⅓ c. water
⅛ t. garlic salt
⅛ t. salt
⅛ t. pepper
½ c. gluten-free green chili sauce
½ c. brown sugar

Put pork, water, salt, garlic salt, and pepper in slow cooker. Cover and cook on high 4 hours. (While pork is cooking, prepare cooked rice and salad dressing.) Drain and shred pork. Stir together the green chili sauce and brown sugar. Add to cooked pork.

1 gluten-free corn tortilla per serving
⅓ c. Mexican blend grated cheese per tortilla
Cooked rice
Lettuce
Fritos® or other gluten-free corn chips
Black beans (chilled and drained)
Corn (chilled and drained)
Fresh salsa (see recipe on next page, if desired)
Sweet pork

When pork and rice are done, melt ⅓ c. cheese on each corn tortilla in the oven or in a frying pan until corn tortilla is crispy. Top tortilla with remaining ingredients and add dressing. (Prepare ingredient quantities above according to number of people being served. Freeze leftover pork.)

(Continued on next page)

Tasty Mexican Salad, Cont'd.

Dressing:

½ Anaheim pepper (remove seeds using gloves, if desired)
½ jalapeno pepper (remove seeds using gloves, if desired
1 ½ cloves garlic or 1 ½ t. minced garlic
2 medium tomatilla tomatoes (roasted or sautéed)
Juice of one lime
Salt, to taste
16 oz. bottle of gluten-free peppercorn ranch dressing

Combine ingredients in blender and mix at high speed. Add lime juice, salt, and peppercorn ranch dressing and blend until well-mixed.

Fresh Salsa

5 medium tomatoes, finely chopped
¼ c. onion, finely chopped
½ c. celery, finely chopped
¼ c. green bell pepper, finely chopped
3 T. canned green chilies, diced
1 ½ T. apple cider vinegar
1 t. mustard seed
1 t. coriander seed, crushed
1 t. salt
⅛ t. pepper

Combine all ingredients and serve.

Makes 10-12 servings.

Cucumbers with Vinegar

*This recipe is only for those who love a sour and salty vinegar flavor.

1 large cucumber
½ c. apple cider vinegar
½ c. water
½ t. garlic salt
½ t. salt

Peel and slice cucumber. Combine other ingredients in a small serving bowl. Add sliced cucumber. Marinate for several hours before serving. Makes 2-3 servings.

Macaroni Salad

½ pkg. **Tinkyada® Elbow Noodles**
¾ c. mayonnaise
½ t. apple cider vinegar
½ t. mustard
1 t. sugar
½ t. garlic salt
⅛ t. pepper
1 stalk celery, chopped (optional)
½ onion or 2 green onions, chopped
2 hard cooked eggs, diced
1 dill pickle, finely diced

Cook elbow noodles until tender. Combine next 6 ingredients in a small bowl and add to drained noodles. Add celery, onion, eggs, and pickles to sauce and noodles and stir well. Mix well again before serving. Makes 5-7 servings.

Favorite Potato Salad

2 hard cooked eggs, diced
5 medium red potatoes, cooked and diced
1 c. mayonnaise
1 t. apple cider vinegar
½ t. mustard
1 t. sugar
¼ t. salt
½ t. garlic salt
¼ t. pepper
¼ t. garlic powder
¼ t. onion powder, to taste
1 c. chopped celery
¼ c. chopped green onions, with green tops

Cover 2 eggs with water (water should cover eggs at least 1 inch.) Bring water to a boil. Turn heat down to medium. Cook eggs for 20 minutes. Drain water and allow eggs to cool before peeling and chopping. Steam or boil red potatoes until tender. Dice into small pieces. Combine next nine ingredients in a large bowl. Add diced potatoes, eggs, chopped celery, and green onions and mix well. Makes 5-7 servings.

Bean Salad

1 can cut green beans, drained
1 can cut yellow wax beans, drained
1 can red kidney beans or garbanzo beans, drained
1 green pepper, diced
1 small onion, diced

Dressing:

¾ c. sugar
⅔ c. vinegar
⅓ c. canola oil
2 T. brown sugar
Lemon pepper, to taste
Garlic salt, to taste

Pour drained beans into a large bowl. Add diced vegetables and mix well. Combine dressing ingredients and add mixture to beans and vegetables. Stir well. Allow dressing to marinate over beans for 8-10 hours. Serve salad using a slotted spoon. Pinto beans can also be added, and dressing recipe can be increased to accomodate more beans. Makes 8-10 servings.

Pretzel Salad

2 ⅔ c. coarsely crushed Ener-G® Foods Crisp Pretzels
3 T. sugar
¾ c. butter

Preheat oven to 350 degrees. Cream the sugar and butter. Add pretzels and mix with spoon. Press into 9" X 13" pan and bake for 10 minutes, and then allow pretzel crust to cool.

8 oz. cream cheese
1 c. sugar or less
4 oz. carton whipped topping

Combine together and spread over pretzel mixture. Refrigerate.

1 large box raspberry or strawberry gelatin
2 c. boiling water
1 pint frozen raspberries or strawberries

Dissolve gelatin in boiling water. Add berries. When partially set, spoon gelatin and fruit mixture over cream cheese mixture. Best if made the day before it is served. Makes 9-11 servings.

Creamy Gelatin Salad

1 small box of raspberry gelatin
1 small box of vanilla pudding (not instant)
2 ½ c. water
8 oz. whipped topping
1 c. fresh strawberries

Cook gelatin, pudding, and water until it boils for 1 minute. Transfer to serving bowl and allow to set up in fridge for 1-2 hours. Add whipped topping and fruit. Makes 5-7 servings.

Mandarin Orange Salad

1 small box of orange gelatin
1 small box of vanilla pudding (not instant)
1 small box of tapioca pudding (not instant)
3 c. water
12 oz. whipped topping
2 small cans of Mandarin oranges

Place gelatin and pudding in large pan. Add water and bring to a boil for one minute, stirring often. Cool mixture in large mixing bowl in the fridge for 1-2 hours. Add whipped topping and oranges. Makes 8-10 servings.

Parmesan Noodles

¼ lb. bacon, cut into pieces, or 2 T. pre-cooked bacon pieces
3 T. butter or margarine
2 cloves (or ½ t.) crushed garlic
⅓ c. Parmesan cheese
¼ c. chopped green onions
½ of 16 oz. pkg. gluten-free spaghetti or spiral noodles
Garlic salt, to taste
1 egg

Cook bacon, pour off grease. (If using pre-cooked bacon pieces, disregard this step and add the pre-cooked bacon to the butter). Add butter and heat with bacon until butter melts. Add garlic and sauté. Remove from heat. Meanwhile, in a small bowl, mix egg, Parmesan cheese, and green onions together. Set aside. Cook the spaghetti noodles until done. Drain noodles and return them to the pan. Immediately add the Parmesan and egg mixture. Heat noodles until the egg is cooked. Add the bacon, garlic, and butter mixture to the noodles and mix well. Makes 5-7 servings.

Creamy Italian Pasta

½ c. onion, chopped
2 cloves crushed garlic, or 1 t. minced garlic
2 T. olive oil
3-4 slices of bacon, or 4 T. bacon pieces
1 large chicken breast
⅔ c. gluten-free spaghetti sauce
1 c. heavy whipping cream
1 t. basil leaves
¼ t. parsley
¼ t. oregano leaves
½ t. salt
¼ t. pepper
16 oz. gluten-free spiral or fettuccini noodles
Parmesan cheese, to taste
Garlic salt, to taste
1-2 c. fried or steamed garden vegetables (optional)
½ c. sliced, fried mushrooms (optional)

(Wait to cook the pasta until the ingredients for the sauce are combined.) In a skillet, sauté the garlic and onion in olive oil. Cut raw chicken and bacon into small pieces and add. Cook on medium until fully cooked and the chicken has no pink color. Pour the sauce and heavy cream over the meat and onion. Mix well. Season with basil, parsley, oregano leaves, and salt and pepper to taste. Simmer the sauce on low for at least 15 minutes, while the water for the pasta boils and the pasta cooks. Strain the pasta and top with sauce and Parmesan cheese, if desired. Add garlic salt, if needed. Add cooked garden vegetables and mushrooms, if desired. Makes 8-10 servings.

Gluten-free Mac and Cheese

½ pkg. gluten-free elbow noodles
¼ c. butter
2 T. milk
1 ½ cheese packets from Kraft Macaroni and Cheese®
(Do not eat noodles included in the box)

Cook the gluten-free noodles. Add butter, milk, and powdered cheese. Makes 3-5 servings.

Tip:

Place the M & C noodles in a plastic bag and give them to a friend who can have food with gluten in it. They can use the noodles for soup.

Roasted Red Potatoes

5-6 red potatoes
4 T. olive oil
1 T. dried parsley
Garlic salt, to taste
Onion salt, to taste
Pepper, to taste

Preheat oven to 425 degrees. Cut cleaned potatoes into wedges. Spread 2 T. of oil over a shallow pan or jelly roll cookie sheet. Place the potatoes in a plastic bag with 2 T. oil. Squeeze and shake the bag until the oil coats the potatoes. Spread the potatoes into a single layer onto the cookie sheet. Sprinkle with seasonings and parsley. Bake for 30-40 minutes or until tender. Makes 5-7 servings.

Garlic Variation

8 small red potatoes, washed
3 T. butter
3 fresh garlic cloves, crushed
Onion Salt, to taste
Garlic Salt, to taste

Steam the red potatoes until tender. Allow to cool slightly. Cut into large cubes, leaving skins on the red potatoes. Melt butter in a large frying pan. Add crushed garlic. Carefully add potatoes to hot butter and garlic. Sprinkle with garlic salt and onion salt. Cook potatoes until lightly browned. Makes 5-7 servings.

Creamy Potatoes

5 potatoes
3 T. butter
½ c. grated cheese
½ c. cream
Salt and pepper
Parsley

Peel potatoes and slice them into French fries. Place foil over a baking sheet with edges, such as a jelly roll cookie sheet. Place sliced potatoes on foil. Cut butter into small pieces and drop them onto the potatoes. Pour cream over all and sprinkle with cheese. Season potatoes with salt and pepper and lightly cover them with parsley. Place a piece of foil over the potatoes and connect the 2 pieces of foil by folding and sealing the edges together. Bake at 425 degrees for 50-55 minutes, or until potatoes are tender. Makes 6-8 servings.

Tasty Yams

2 medium-sized yams
½ c. brown sugar
⅓ c. butter
1 c. miniature marshmallows (optional)

Scrub yams until skins are clean. Pierce skins of each yam with a knife. Microwave for 7-10 minutes, or until yams indent slightly when squeezed. Cut yams in half and remove cooked yams from skins. Place them in an 8" X 8" glass casserole dish. Press yams with a fork until all lumps are removed. Add brown sugar and butter. Microwave for 2-4 minutes, or until butter melts and brown sugar dissolves. Mix well. If marshmallows are desired, cover yams with the marshmallows and broil the yams in the oven until marshmallows turn light brown. Do not leave oven unattended, since this process happens very quickly. Makes 4-6 servings.

Fried Zucchini

1 large zucchini
1 egg
1 t. water
¼ c. rice flour
¼ c. corn flour or cornmeal
Canola oil
Garlic salt, to taste
Seasoned salt, to taste

Peel zucchini and cut into ⅛"-¼" slices. Combine egg and water in a sealable bag. Add zucchini and squeeze and shake bag until egg and water coats the zucchini. Mix rice flour and corn flour (or cornmeal) together in a pie plate. Dip both sides of each zucchini slice in flour mixture. Fry zucchini on griddle coated with canola oil until zucchini is golden brown on each side. Season with garlic salt and seasoned salt. Makes 6-8 servings.

Apple Dip

4 Fuji apples
8 oz. cream cheese
1 ¼ c. brown sugar
1 t. vanilla

Wash and slice apples. In a serving bowl, combine cream
cheese, brown sugar, and vanilla. Whip with a spoon or
electric mixer until smooth and creamy. Dip apples in mixture.
Makes 4-6 servings.

El Salvadoran Rice

1 c. white, long grain rice (not instant rice)
¼ c. canola oil
2 c. water
½ t. gluten-free chicken bouillon
1 small onion, diced
2 carrots, grated
1 t. salt
¼ t. garlic salt
1 tomato, chopped
2 T. cilantro, chopped
Onion salt, to taste

Place rice in frying pan with ¼ cup oil. Stir until oil is absorbed and rice is browned slightly. Add water, bouillon, onion, carrots, salt, and garlic salt. Reduce heat to low, cover with lid, and simmer for 20-30 minutes. Taste the rice and if it is not soft and tender, add more water and bouillon and simmer the rice for additional time. Add chopped tomatoes and cilantro before serving. Season with onion salt, to taste. Makes 3-5 servings.

Spanish Rice

1 c. raw white or brown rice, or a mixture of both (not quick rice)
2 c. hot water
2 T. canola oil
½ c. chopped onion
½ c. chopped bell pepper
¼ c. carrots, thinly sliced or grated
1 clove garlic, minced
¼ t. cumin
1 t. salt
⅛ t. black pepper
1 c. chopped, fresh tomatoes
Fresh cilantro (optional)
Lime juice, to taste (optional)
Garlic salt, to taste

Preheat oven to 350 degrees. Pour 1 c. raw rice and 2 c. water into buttered or sprayed 9" X 9" casserole dish covered with foil. Bake for 50-60 minutes, or until water is absorbed. While rice is baking, sauté the onion, carrots, and green bell pepper in canola oil until tender. Add minced garlic and seasonings. Place baked rice in frying pan with 2 T. oil and stir well to coat with oil. Add cooked vegetables and seasonings. Heat rice mixture for several more minutes. Add raw tomatoes and desired optional ingredients. Sprinkle with garlic salt. Makes 4-6 servings.

Fried Rice

1 ½ c. raw white rice (not quick rice)
1 ½ c. raw brown rice (not quick rice)
6 c. water
Canola oil
½ t. crushed garlic
2 eggs
3 green onions
Ground ginger, to taste
Garlic salt, to taste
Onion salt, to taste

Preheat oven to 350 degrees. Spray a 9" x 13" casserole dish with cooking spray. In addition, pour a thin layer of canola oil across the bottom of the dish. Pour rice and water into dish. Cover with foil. Bake for 1 hour to 1 hour and 20 minutes, or until water is absorbed. It is easier to work with the rice if it has cooled slightly or completely before you place it in the frying pan or wok.

Pour olive or canola oil across large non-stick frying pan or wok, until the bottom of the pan is covered. Add crushed garlic, eggs, and chopped green onions and stir them together as you scramble the eggs. Add the cooked rice. Sprinkle all with a small amount of ground ginger. Sprinkle with garlic salt and onion salt and mix well. Fry until rice is completely warmed. Makes 7-9 servings.

*The sweet and sour sauce included in the recipe for "Sweet and Sour Meatballs" is delicious served with this rice.

Ham Fried Rice

½ c. raw white rice (not quick rice)
½ c. raw brown rice (not quick rice)
1 c. water
1 c. chicken broth
½ t. salt
¼ t. gluten-free chicken bouillon
⅛ c. butter

Preheat oven to 350 degrees. Combine ingredients in a covered glass 9" X 9" baking pan or casserole dish covered with foil, for 45-50 minutes, or until rice is free of liquid. Allow rice to cool slightly while working on ham and vegetables.

1 c. diced, cooked ham, or 3 T. gluten-free bacon pieces
⅓ c. butter or canola oil
½ c. chopped onion
¼ c. chopped green pepper
¼ c. diced celery
½ c. sliced mushrooms (optional)
2 t. gluten-free soy sauce

Cook above ingredients in a large non-stick frying pan until vegetables are tender. Add about three-fourths of the cooked rice to the vegetables and mix well.

Move the rice and vegetable mixture to the side of the pan and place 1 egg in the empty part of the pan. Stir until the egg is scrambled. Blend the pieces of the cooked egg into the reserved one-fourth portion of rice. Combine all of rice together. Makes 4-6 servings.

Option: Add 1 cup of very finely shredded Chinese cabbage.

Italian Rice

4 c. cooked rice
½ t. crushed garlic
1 c. gluten-free spaghetti sauce
½ t. garlic salt
½ c. grated cheese
1 T. Parmesan cheese

Combine all and heat in microwave until warm. Top with additional Parmesan cheese, if desired. Makes 6-8 servings.

Another Italian Rice (Zesty)

Gluten-free Italian Salad Dressing
Butter
Lemon juice
Garlic salt
Cooked rice

Add first four ingredients to cooked rice, according to taste.

Red Spanish Rice

1 medium onion, diced (or 1 T. dried, minced onion)
1 small green pepper, diced
2 garlic cloves, crushed (or 1 t. minced garlic)
2 T. canola oil
2 c. uncooked rice
4 c. water
1 t. gluten-free beef bouillon
14.5 oz. can diced or stewed tomatoes
1 T. brown sugar
⅛ t. hot red pepper sauce
1 t. salt
¼ t. pepper
1 ½ t. chili powder
½ t. cumin
1 T. gluten-free Worcestershire sauce
2-3 T. chopped cilantro
Shredded Cheese
Sour Cream

Saute onion, green pepper, and garlic until tender in a large frying pan coated with 2 T. oil. Add uncooked rice and mix well. Add remaining ingredients and mix well. Bring to a boil and then turn heat to medium. Simmer for 30 minutes. If rice is not tender, add more chicken broth or water and simmer the rice for additional time. Serve with grated cheese and sour cream. Makes 5-7 servings.

Chinese Fried Rice

4 c. cooked rice, cooled
1 egg
½ t. water
2 T. canola oil
½ c. cooked diced ham, cooked chicken, or cooked pork
1 t. minced garlic
1 can mushrooms, or ½ c. fresh mushrooms (optional)
2 T. green onions, finely chopped
2 ½ T. gluten-free soy sauce
½ T. butter

Cook rice and set aside to cool. Beat egg and water in a small bowl. Using a non-stick frying pan, coat surface of pan with egg. Cook until light brown. Remove from pan and cut into small strips. Pour oil into large frying pan. Fry meat until heated through. Add garlic, mushrooms, green onions, soy sauce, and butter. Mix well. Add rice and mix well. Cook for 10 minutes over low heat. Add cooked eggs and cook for 5 additional minutes. Makes 6-8 servings.

Mary Beth, age 47

I wasn't too concerned about having celiac disease when my parents and siblings were encouraging me to get tested. I had been healthy and really didn't think I had any symptoms related to the disease. Because of the strong hereditary tendencies, however, I didn't mind being tested.

I was in my 40's. I was starting to feel like some of the age-related health issues were catching up to me. For example, I was beginning to have a lot of joint pain in my hips and hands. I worried that it was the beginning of arthritis problems similar to what my Mom had suffered with for years. I had also noticed my stools often were oily and I had increased flatulence.

Because I thought these things were age-related, I was very surprised when the blood test showed positive for celiac disease. I then followed the diet for a few weeks to see if it would make any difference. I was amazed when I had a bowl of cornflakes (no wheat, just barley extract) and immediately had a stomach ache.

After being on the diet for awhile, I realized that the joint pain was gone and other symptoms were markedly improved. Another interesting and happy side effect that I didn't expect from following the diet, was that I was sleeping better than I had in years. I have felt it is worth the effort to follow the diet to avoid the immediate side effects and uncomfortable symptoms now, and to prevent the bigger health problems that can happen later, such as arthritis, osteoporosis and cancer.

Main Dishes

Pineapple Chicken Lo Mien

1 can pineapple chunks, with ⅓ c. juice reserved
1 lb. chicken, diced
2 cloves garlic, minced
¾ t. ginger
2 T. canola oil
2 medium carrots, thinly sliced
1 medium green pepper, chopped (optional)
1 pkg. Thai Kitchen® Thin Rice Noodles or Tinkyada® Spaghetti Noodles
3 green onions, sliced
1 T. cornstarch
⅓ c. gluten-free soy sauce
1 T. canola oil

Drain pineapple, reserving ⅓ c. juice. Set aside. Cook chicken, garlic, and ginger in oil until chicken begins to brown. Add carrots and green pepper. Cover and cook until vegetables and chicken are done. Cook noodles. Stir in drained noodles and green onions. Combine cornstarch, soy sauce, and pineapple juice with 1 T. oil. Stir into chicken mixture. Cook for 2 min. until sauce is thickened. Add pineapple, if desired. Makes 6-8 servings.

Hot and Spicy Chicken

4 boneless, skinless chicken breasts, sliced in thin strips
¼ c. cornstarch
2 T. corn flour
2 c. brown sugar
½ c. Frank's® Original Red Hot® Sauce
Canola oil

Slice chicken into strips. Place cornstarch and corn flour in a plastic bag and mix. Place chicken in the bag and shake to cover chicken. Coat the bottom of a non-stick frying pan with canola oil. Brown chicken until cooked. Combine brown sugar and hot sauce in a glass measuring cup. Microwave until sugar is dissolved, around 2 minutes. Add heated sauce to chicken and warm over medium heat for several minutes. Makes 5-7 servings.

Tip:

Chicken breasts are more easily sliced if partially frozen.

Chinese Noodles

4 bone-in chicken breasts
Garlic salt
Onion salt
Black pepper or lemon pepper
2 T. onion or green onions, chopped
6 hard-cooked eggs
1 pkg. Tinkyada Spaghetti Noodles, cooked
Gluten-free soy sauce

Pour water into large pot. Add uncooked chicken breasts and seasonings. Water should cover chicken while cooking. Cook until chicken is tender, approximately 2-3 hours for thawed, larger bone-in chicken. Reserve the broth to serve with noodles.

Place eggs in a saucepan. Cover eggs with water (water should cover eggs at least 1 inch.) Bring water to a boil. Turn heat down to medium. Cook eggs for 20 minutes. Drain water and cover eggs with cold water. Allow eggs to cool before peeling and slicing.

Cook the spaghetti noodles. Cut or tear the chicken into small pieces. Strain broth from the cooked chicken into a serving dish. Each person being served places noodles, broth, chicken, eggs, and onions into their individual soup bowls. Add soy sauce to taste. Makes 6-8 servings.

Japanese Style Chicken

3 large boneless chicken breasts, sliced in thin strips
⅓ c. gluten-free soy sauce
¼ c. brown sugar
½ t. crushed garlic
½ t. powdered ginger
¼ t. toasted sesame oil
Sesame Seeds to cover chicken
Cooked rice
Corn tortillas, optional

Brown the chicken in oil until nearly done. Combine soy sauce, brown sugar, garlic, ginger, and sesame oil. Pour over the chicken and completely cook the chicken over medium heat. Serve with cooked rice. Another option is to make a wrap-up. Place pieces of chicken and a spoonful of cooked rice in a warm tortilla. To warm the tortillas, surround them in a moist paper towel or wrap them in a clean dish towel. Place them in the microwave until they are soft and pliable, approximately 45 seconds for 2 tortillas. Makes 3-5 servings.

Tip:

This chicken recipe is delicious when the chicken is cooked on a grill. Marinate the chicken in sauce for several hours before grilling.

Chicken Strips

4 boneless, skinless chicken breasts
¼ c. cornstarch
2 T. corn flour
2 T. canola oil
Garlic salt, to taste
Onion salt, to taste
Lemon pepper, to taste

Partially thaw chicken breasts. Slice chicken into strips. Place cornstarch and corn flour in a plastic bag and mix them together. Place chicken in the bag and shake to cover chicken. Coat the bottom of a non-stick frying pan with canola oil. Fry chicken on both sides until browned and thoroughly cooked. Add more oil, as needed. Add garlic salt, onion salt, and lemon pepper, to taste. Makes 4-5 servings.

Baked Whole Chicken

1 whole chicken*
Water
Garlic Salt
Onion Salt

Preheat oven to 425 degrees. Place chicken in glass baking dish. Add water to barely cover the bottom of the dish. Sprinkle garlic salt and onion salt on top of the chicken. Bake uncovered at 425 degrees for ½ hour and then cover chicken with foil and bake it at 350 degrees for 1 hour, or until chicken is cooked completely. To determine if chicken is completely cooked, poke a fork or sharp knife into the thickest part of the chicken and ensure that the broth is clear. Makes 5-7 servings.

*Check to make sure there is no broth with wheat in it injected into the chicken. Also, check the ingredients if the chicken has seasoning on it.

Tip:

Chicken may also be placed in an oven bag before baking, with water or broth added to the bag.

Quick Chicken Tortillas

2 corn tortillas for each serving
Chicken, cooked and cubed
Bacon, cooked and crumbled
Cheese, grated
Onions, diced
Cilantro, chopped without stems
Canned green chilies (optional)
Tomatoes, diced
Salsa, fresh or canned
Sour Cream

Butter one side of one tortilla per serving. Put butter side down in non-stick frying pan. Cover the tortilla with small portions of each of the other ingredients, except tomatoes, salsa, and sour cream. Butter one side of the second tortilla and place it, butter side up, on the covered tortilla in the pan. Lightly brown tortilla using medium heat until cheese melts. Turn over tortilla stack and brown the second buttered tortilla. Serve with tomatoes, salsa, and sour cream.

Tip:

Warming the tortillas in the microwave keeps them from breaking up. This will help the butter to spread more easily.

BBQ Chicken

4-5 boneless, skinless chicken breasts
1 ½ T. gluten-free Worcestershire sauce
¾ c. grape jelly
1 ½ c. ketchup
3 T. mustard
1 clove minced garlic

Preheat oven to 350 degrees. Place chicken breasts in 9" X 13" sprayed casserole dish. Combine ingredients for sauce and pour over chicken. Cover and bake chicken for 1 hour. Makes 4-5 servings.

Another BBQ Sauce

1 bottle gluten-free honey barbeque sauce
½ c. ketchup
2 ½ T. gluten-free Worcestershire sauce
⅔ c. brown sugar
½ c. onion, diced
1 ½ T. butter
1 c. gluten-free smoked sausage, sliced
8 chicken legs and thighs (or 6-7 cooked boneless, skinless chicken breasts prepared as chicken strips)

Combine barbeque sauce, ketchup, Worcestershire sauce, and brown sugar in a medium bowl. Dice onion and sauté in butter until tender in a large frying pan. Add sauce and sausage. Simmer for 2 hours. Pour over chicken legs and thighs and bake at 350 degrees in a covered casserole dish for 1 hour or more. Or prepare and cook chicken strips (use recipe on P. 98) and pour simmered sauce over them before serving. Makes 6-8 servings.

Salt and Vinegar Chicken

8 chicken thighs or drumsticks (no boneless, skinless pieces)
1 c. apple cider vinegar
2 T. salt, approximately
Cooking oil

Preheat oven to 425 degrees. Place the vinegar in a heavy plastic bag. Add salt and close the bag. Squeeze and shake the bag until the salt dissolves in the vinegar. Place the pieces of chicken in the bag with the salt-vinegar solution and squeeze and shake the mixture over the chicken.

Place the chicken in a glass casserole dish or metal cake pan that has been lined with aluminum foil and then covered with cooking oil. (The chicken tends to stick to the baking dish, even with the coating of oil. The aluminum foil reduces the difficulty as you clean the dish.) Bake for 1 hour or more, un-covered. The salty, crisp skin is delicious. To ensure a clean oven, an alternate cooking method is to place the chicken in a plastic oven bag before baking. The skin won't be crispy, however. Makes 6-8 servings.

Tip:

Many types of vinegar are gluten-free due to the distilling process where protein is removed. Apple cider vinegar works well in recipes.

Creamy Chicken Enchiladas

4 boneless, skinless chicken breasts
⅓ c. butter
⅓ c. rice flour
3 c. chicken broth
1 t. - 1 ½ T. jalapeno pepper (optional)
1 ½ c. sour cream
12-14 gluten-free corn tortillas
2 c. grated cheese

Preheat oven to 350 degrees. Bake chicken for approximately 1 hour in a covered casserole dish, with enough water to cover the bottom of the dish. Cut cooked chicken into cubes, and place in large bowl. In a medium saucepan, melt the butter. Stir in rice flour. Gradually pour in chicken broth. Add jalapeno pepper, if desired. Bring to a boil until slightly thickened. Remove from heat and add sour cream. Mix sauce well with a whisk. Pour about ½ c. sauce across the bottom of a greased 9" X 13" baking pan or glass casserole dish. Pour half of remaining sauce into the bowl with the cubed chicken. Mix well.

Surround the stack of tortillas in a moist paper towel or wrap them in a clean dish towel. Place them in the microwave until they are soft and pliable, approximately 2 minutes for 12 tortillas. Allow tortillas to cool slightly. Cup each tortilla in your hand and place a spoonful of chicken and sauce mixture down the center of the tortilla. Roll the tortilla around the mixture and place each one side by side in casserole dish. Cover rolled tortillas with the other half of the sauce and grated cheese. Bake at 350 degrees for 30 minutes. Makes 6-8 servings.

*The sauce for this recipe is also delicious when combined with cooked, diced ham and served over baked potatoes.

Red Sauce Creamy Enchiladas

4 boneless, skinless or bone-in whole chicken breasts
½ t. salt
1 t. garlic salt
1 t. lemon pepper
1 t. chicken bouillon
1 T. minced, dried onion
6 c. water

Pour water into large pot. Add uncooked chicken breasts and seasonings. Water should cover chicken during the cooking. Cook until chicken is tender, approximately one hour for thawed boneless chicken breasts, and 2-3 hours for thawed bone-in chicken. Cut or tear the chicken into small pieces. Strain 4 cups of broth from the cooked chicken and pour into a saucepan.

Make a creamy sauce with the following:
¼ c. cornstarch
½ c. cold water
4 c. of broth in saucepan (see above)
1 c. sour cream
1 small can green chilies

Mix cornstarch into cup of water until smooth. Add cornstarch and water mixture to strained broth. Bring to a boil over medium high heat, while stirring vigorously. Remove from heat. Add sour cream and green chilies.

(Continued on next page)

Red Sauce Creamy Enchiladas, Continued

12-14 corn tortillas, 6 or 8 inch size
1 small can red enchilada sauce (check label, or use reduced quantity of sauce recipe included with "Beef Enchiladas")
1 ½ c. grated cheese
Sliced black olives, optional
1 large tomato, diced
2 c. shredded lettuce
Salsa
Sour cream

Heat a small amount of oil in a fry pan with a non-stick surface. Dip corn tortillas in the oil on both sides to soften them. Allow tortilla to cool slightly. Dip tortilla in a pie plate full of enchilada sauce, covering both sides with sauce. Then cup the tortilla in your hand and place chicken pieces down the center of the tortilla, as well as a large spoonful of sauce, a line of grated cheese, and sliced black olives (if desired). Fold the tortilla over in half and layer them, overlapping, in a greased 9" x 13" baking pan or glass casserole dish. Cover folded tortillas with the rest of the sauce and additional grated cheese. Bake at 350 degrees until bubbling. Serve with fresh salsa, shredded lettuce, chopped tomatoes, and slightly thinned sour cream. Makes 6-8 servings.

Tip:

For an easier (but less authentic) Mexican enchilada, you may prefer to use tortillas warmed in the microwave, instead of warmed in hot oil.

Sweet and Sour Chicken

¾ c. sugar
¼ c. pineapple juice
½ c. apple cider vinegar
3 T. ketchup
1 T. soy sauce
½ t. salt
4-5 chicken breasts, boneless and skinless, cut in strips
¼ c. cornstarch
Canola oil

Combine the first six ingredients and simmer in a saucepan. Meanwhile, dip chicken in cornstarch or shake the chicken in a bag with cornstarch. Fry the chicken in canola oil until browned and cooked through. Pour heated sauce over chicken and heat until sauce is slightly thickened. Chicken can also be fried until browned, placed in a casserole dish, covered with sauce, and baked at 350 degrees for 50-60 minutes. Makes 4-6 servings.

Lemon Chicken

4 boneless, skinless chicken breasts, sliced in thin strips
¼ c. cornstarch
2 T. corn flour
2 T. butter
Canola oil
Garlic salt, to taste

Slice chicken into strips. Place cornstarch and corn flour in a plastic bag and mix. Place chicken in the bag and shake to cover chicken. Coat the bottom of a non-stick frying pan with butter and add canola oil, as needed. Brown the chicken until it is completely cooked. Add garlic salt, to taste.

Meanwhile, combine the following in a blender (or in a glass measuring cup and use a hand blender):

⅓ c. sugar
2 T. fresh lemon juice
1 t. canola oil
½ t. pepper
2 t. cornstarch
¼ t. crushed garlic
1 t. chicken bouillon

Pour onto chicken and fry until sauce thickens. Makes 4-6 servings.

Alternate Sour Sauce for Lemon Chicken

1 t. dried oregano
½ t. gluten-free seasoned salt
¼ t. pepper
1 t. fresh or dried parsley

¼ c. water
3 T. lemon juice
1 t. crushed garlic
1 t. gf chicken bouillon

Hawaiian Haystacks

2-4 bone-in chicken breasts
1 small onion, sliced into large pieces
2 stalks celery, sliced into large pieces
1 t. gluten-free chicken bouillon
1 t. salt
1 t. pepper
½ t. garlic salt

Place chicken in a large pot and cover it with water. Add remaining ingredients and gently boil chicken in water for 2 to 3 hours until the chicken is tender. Add more water as needed. (After 1 hour of simmering, begin rice preparation. See directions below.) Remove chicken when fully cooked and allow it to cool slightly. Cut the chicken into cubes. Strain the chicken broth into a quart size measuring cup and set it aside for gravy. Discard the onions and celery.

½ c. raw white rice (not quick rice)
½ c. raw brown rice (not quick rice)
1 c. water
1 c. chicken broth
½ t. salt
¼ t. gluten-free chicken bouillon
⅛ c. butter

Preheat oven to 350 degrees. Combine ingredients in a covered glass 9" X 9" baking pan or casserole dish covered with foil, for 45-50 minutes, or until rice is free of liquid.

(Continued on next page)

Hawaiian Haystacks, Cont'd.

Reserved chicken broth
Cornstarch
Cold water
Garlic salt, to taste
Onion salt, to taste
Gluten-free chicken bouillon, to taste
Chicken, cooked and cubed
2 tomatoes, diced
2 stalks celery, trimmed and diced
1 small can crushed pineapple
½ c. coconut
1 c. grated cheese

While rice is baking, prepare the chicken gravy by thickening the reserved chicken broth with cornstarch mixed in cold water. Measure out the number of broth used according to the number of people being served. (Plan on around 1 c. of broth per person.) For each cup of broth, dissolve 1 T. of cornstarch in ⅛ c. of cold water. (If more than 1 T. of cornstarch is needed, try dissolving the additional cornstarch in the ⅛ c. of cold water. Add more water 1 t. at a time as needed.) Heat the broth in a saucepan and stir in the cornstarch and water mixture. Boil gently until smooth, clear, and thickened. Taste gravy and add additional seasonings and chicken bouillon, if needed. Add cooked, diced chicken to gravy.

Prepare remaining toppings and place each of the ingredients in separate dishes. Each person will build their own "haystack" beginning with rice, chicken and gravy, and various desired toppings. Makes 1 serving/cup of broth.

Chicken or Shrimp Stir-Fry

2 c. cooked, cubed chicken and/or
1 - 1 ½ lbs. cooked shrimp
1 stalk celery, sliced
2 carrots, grated
1 c. chopped onion
1 can water chestnuts (optional)
1 c. chicken broth
2 T. + 1 t. cornstarch
½ t. minced garlic
½ t. ground ginger
2 T. gluten-free soy sauce
1 ½ t. sugar
1 c. pea pods
1 c. fresh, sliced mushrooms
Cooked rice or noodles

In a non-stick frying pan, sauté the celery, carrots, and onion in oil over medium heat until tender. Add shrimp (and/or cooked chicken) and reduce heat to warm. Combine cornstarch and chicken broth in a small saucepan and heat and stir until clear and smooth. Add garlic, spices, soy sauce, and sugar. Stir until dissolved. Pour over shrimp and vegetables. Stir in mushrooms and pea pods. Serve over rice or gluten-free noodles. Makes 4-6 servings.

Chicken Fettuccine

8 oz. cream cheese
¼ c. butter
½ c. Parmesan cheese
2 c. milk
½ t. garlic powder
¼ t. pepper
5 slices of bacon, cut into small pieces and cooked
1–2 cooked, diced chicken breasts
1 pkg. gluten-free fettuccine noodles, cooked and drained

Place first six ingredients in saucepan and cook until smooth and warm. Set aside to cool and thicken. Fry bacon and chicken. Cook noodles. Gently combine sauce, bacon, and chicken with the cooked noodles. Makes 7-9 servings.

Chicken and Rice with Sweet Lemon Sauce

4-5 boneless, skinless chicken breasts
¼ c. cornstarch
2 T. corn flour
2 T. canola oil
Garlic salt, to taste
Onion salt, to taste
Fried Rice

Begin preparations for Fried Rice (see recipe for "Fried Rice" in this cookbook). Partially thaw chicken breasts. Slice chicken into strips. Place cornstarch and corn flour in a plastic bag and mix them together. Place chicken in the bag and shake to cover chicken. Coat the bottom of a non-stick frying pan with canola oil. Fry chicken in oil until brown and crispy and completely cooked. Add more oil, as needed. Add garlic salt and onion salt, to taste.

Place chicken over cooked fried rice and top with the following sauce:

⅓ c. cornstarch
1 c. sugar
¼ t. salt
¼ c. lemon juice
1 ½ c. boiling water

Combine first four ingredients and then add boiling water. Cook for 1 minute or until thick and clear. Pour sauce over prepared chicken and serve. Extra sauce is delicious served over the fried rice. Makes 4-6 servings.

Thai Red Curry

3 ½ c. cooked rice
2-3 boneless, skinless chicken breasts
1 T. canola oil
4 crushed garlic cloves (or 1 t.)
1 t. ground ginger
1 onion, thinly sliced
2 carrots, sliced
1 green or red bell pepper, diced
14 oz. can coconut milk, or 2 c. cream
1 t. Thai red curry paste
2 T. gluten-free soy sauce
2 T. sugar

Cook rice. Slice chicken into strips. Sauté the chicken, onion, garlic, and ginger in canola oil until cooked. Remove from frying pan and set aside. Sauté carrots and peppers until tender. Add coconut milk (or cream), curry paste, soy sauce and sugar. Stir well and add chicken and onion mixture and simmer 3-4 minutes. Serve over cooked rice or add rice to the Thai Red Curry until liquid absorbs into the rice. Makes 4-6 servings.

Chinese Sweet and Sour

Cooked rice
1 pound meat of your choice, cubed
1 T. olive oil
½ c. chopped green peppers
1 can pineapple tidbits, drained
1 can Mandarin oranges, save ¼ c. juice, drain the rest

Sauce:

1 c. water
¼ c. honey
¼ c. sugar
½ c. ketchup
1 c. brown sugar
¼ c. vinegar
1 T. gluten-free soy sauce
¼ c. juice from Mandarin oranges
3 T. cornstarch

Brown meat and add peppers the last 2-3 min. of cooking meat. Reserve juice from Mandarin oranges. Add pineapple and Mandarin oranges to meat. Cover and set off the hot burner. Combine first seven ingredients of sauce in separate pan. Bring to a boil. Mix cornstarch with the reserved fruit juice and add to boiling liquid. Let boil on medium heat until thick, about 2-3 minutes. Add to cooked meat mixture. Serve with cooked rice. Makes 6-8 servings.

Parmesan Cheese Chicken

4 chicken breasts
1 egg, mixed well with 1 t. water
½ c. gluten-free bread crumbs, sprinkled lightly with poultry seasoning
¼ c. Parmesan cheese
⅛ t. paprika
¼ t. Italian seasoning
¼ t. salt
¼ t. pepper
Sliced ham (optional)
Sliced cheese (optional)

Preheat oven to 350 degrees. Dip chicken in egg. Combine remaining ingredients in pie plate. Dip chicken in bread crumb mixture. Place on greased cookie sheet. For easy clean-up, place a piece of foil on cookie sheet and spray foil with cooking spray. Bake for 50-60 minutes. If desired, cover cooked chicken with slices of ham and cheese. Continue baking for 2-3 minutes until cheese melts for a Chicken Cordon Bleu. Makes 4 servings.

Serve chicken with the following sauce:

½ t. mustard
3 T. mayonnaise

Mix together in small serving bowl.

Honey Mustard Chicken

4 chicken breasts
¼ c. cornstarch
2 T. corn flour
2 T. canola oil
Garlic salt, to taste
Onion salt, to taste
¼ c. butter
½ c. honey
¼ c. mustard
¼ t. curry powder
¼ t. salt
Cooked rice or noodles

Begin preparations for cooked rice or noodles. Partially thaw chicken breasts. Slice chicken into strips. Place cornstarch and corn flour in a plastic bag and mix them together. Place chicken in the bag and shake to cover chicken. Coat the bottom of a non-stick frying pan with canola oil. Fry chicken in oil until brown and crispy and completely cooked. Add more oil, as needed. Add garlic salt and onion salt, to taste.

Melt the butter and honey over medium heat. Add mustard, curry powder, and salt. Pour over chicken and fry until sauce thickens slightly. Serve with cooked rice or cooked noodles. Makes 4 servings.

Paprika Chicken

½ c. butter
½ c. rice flour
3 ¾ c. milk
1 T. gluten-free chicken bouillon
1 t. paprika
¾ c. sour cream
Garlic salt and onion salt, to taste
2 boneless, skinless chicken breasts, cooked and diced
8-10 baked potatoes

Fry or bake chicken breasts and bake the potatoes. Melt butter in saucepan and add rice flour. Add milk, bouillon, and paprika and cook over medium high heat until thickened. Remove from heat. Add sour cream, garlic salt, onion salt, and cooked chicken. Serve over baked potatoes. Makes 8-10 servings.

Italian Chicken

4 boneless, skinless chicken breasts
1 c. gluten-free spaghetti sauce
1 c. grated mozzarella cheese
Garlic salt, to taste

Preheat oven to 350 degrees. Place chicken breasts in a 9" X 13" casserole dish. Cover with spaghetti sauce and grated cheese. Bake chicken for 1 hour. Add garlic salt, to taste. Makes 4 servings.

Honey Garlic Chicken

4 boneless, skinless chicken breasts
Canola oil
2 t. crushed garlic
¼ t. salt
1 T. apple cider vinegar
2 T. butter
½ c. honey

Optional ingredients for wrap-ups:

Gluten-free corn tortillas
Cooked rice
Ranch dressing
Tomatoes, diced
Avocados, diced

Prepare cooked rice, if desired. Slice chicken into strips. Fry chicken breasts in oil until completely cooked. In a glass measuring cup or small bowl, add garlic, salt, vinegar, butter, and honey. Microwave until combined and pourable. Pour over chicken and fry for several more minutes. Serve by itself or make a wrap-up using a corn tortilla topped with cooked chicken, rice, ranch dressing, tomatoes, and avocados. Makes 4 servings. For wrap-ups, recipe makes 6-8 servings.

Irish Nachos

1 pkg. gluten-free French fries
1 pkg. bacon
2 c. grated cheese
⅓ c. sliced green onions
½ c. diced tomatoes
Ranch dressing or cottage cheese

Bake French fries according to package directions. Fry bacon until crispy and slice into small pieces. Prepare other toppings. Place French fries on serving plate. Top with remaining desired items. Makes 5-7 servings.

Sweet and Sour Pork

4 boneless pork chops
⅓ c. cornstarch
Garlic powder
1 c. sugar
½ c. apple cider vinegar
1 c. chicken broth (or 1 c. water with 1 t. gluten-free chicken bouillon)
⅓ c. ketchup
1 ½ T. gluten-free soy sauce
Cooked rice

Prepare Fried Rice (see P. 87). Preheat oven to 325 degrees. Slice pork into cubes or thin strips. Roll pork in cornstarch (or shake pork in a bag with cornstarch). Place in non-stick skillet and sprinkle with garlic powder. Brown on both sides lightly. Combine sugar, vinegar, chicken broth, ketchup, and soy sauce in a saucepan. Bring to a boil for 2 minutes. Place pork in a 9" x13" baking dish, sprayed with cooking spray. Pour sauce over pork and bake uncovered for 1-1 ½ hours or until pork is cooked through and tender. After 40-45 minutes of baking, check to ensure there is enough liquid and that the sauce is not burning. If needed, add a small amount of chicken broth to sauce to prevent burning. Serve with prepared rice. Makes 4-6 servings.

Seasoned Pork Chops

4-6 pork chops
3 T. rice flour
1 ½ t. dried oregano leaves
1 t. salt
¼ t. pepper
¼ t. garlic powder
2 T. oil
1 can pineapple chunks and juice
¼ c. water
2 T. brown sugar
2 T. dried chopped onion
2 T. ketchup

In a pie plate, combine rice flour, oregano, salt, pepper, and garlic powder. Dip both sides of pork chops in mixture. Pour oil into large frying pan or skillet. Place pork chops in pan and fry until browned. Preheat oven to 350 degrees. Combine pineapple, water, brown sugar, onion, and ketchup in a saucepan and heat until brown sugar dissolves. Transfer pork chops to 9" X 13" casserole dish and pour sauce and pineapple over them. (Or serve pineapple separately instead of heating it.) Bake for 1 to 1 ½ hours. Makes 4-6 servings.

BBQ Pork Chops

4 pork chops
Gluten-free barbeque sauce

Preheat oven to 325 degrees. Pour bottled barbeque sauce over pork chops and bake for approximately 2 hours. Makes 4 servings.

Pork Roast

1 pork roast
3-4 lbs. for a small roast; 5-6 lbs. for a large roast
Canola oil
Salt, pepper, and garlic salt, to taste
1 T. minced, dried onion or 1 small onion, sliced
1 regular size oven bag
2 c. water for small roast; 4 c. water for large roast

Preheat oven to 325 degrees. Brown the roast in a deep, heavy pan with enough oil to cover the bottom of the pan. Open the baking bag and place it in a 9" X 13" casserole dish. Do not place any flour in the bag as instructed by the bag manufacturer. Sprinkle the roast with seasonings and top with onions. Place roast in baking bag.

Pour 2 c. water (or 4 c., depending on size of roast) in the pan used to brown the roast. Stir to make a broth with the juices of the meat.   Add broth to the seasoned roast inside of the baking bag. Close the baking bag with the tie provided and snip 3-4 small slits in the top of the bag.

Bake roast for 3-4 hours, depending on the size and cut of the roast. Makes 6-9 servings.

Old Fashioned Milk Gravy

Pan fry beef sirloin tip steaks, cube steaks, pork chops, or pork cutlets in a heavy frying pan. Season with salt and pepper. Remove cooked meat from the frying pan and skim off excess fat.

½ c. milk, per serving
2 t. cornstarch, per serving
¼ t. of salt and ⅛ t. pepper for each ½ c. milk
Gluten-free chicken or beef bouillon powder, to taste

Using a wire whisk or mixing spring, combine the milk, cornstarch, salt, and pepper in a small bowl. Stir milk mixture into the frying pan. Stir constantly while cooking on medium heat until thickened. Add additional milk or thickening, if needed, for desired consistency. Season gravy to taste with bouillon powder.

Sweet Pear Pork Chops

5-6 thin pork chops
3 T. rice flour
1 ½ t. dried oregano leaves, crushed
1 t. salt
¼ t. pepper
¼ t. garlic powder
Canola oil
1 c. pear juice
⅓ c. water
2 T. brown sugar
1 T. + 1 t. cornstarch

Trim excess fat from meat. In a shallow dish, mix rice flour, oregano leaves, salt, pepper, and garlic powder. Coat the pork chops on both sides using all of the mixture. In a skillet, fry chops on both sides in canola oil until completely cooked. Or transfer pork chops to 9" X 13" casserole dish with ½ c. water. Bake at 325 degrees for 1 to 1 ½ hours, or until fully cooked. Remove pork chops from the casserole dish and place on a serving platter. Prepare the sauce by combining the last four ingredients and bringing to a boil until thickened. Pour over cooked pork chops. Makes 5-6 servings.

Easy Vegetable Noodle Casserole

7 link sausages (or 1 c. cooked ground sausage)
1 bag frozen vegetables, or 3-4 c. fresh vegetables
1 package Thai Kitchen® Instant Noodle Soup-Spring Onion
¾ c. grated cheese

Preheat oven to 350 degrees. Cook and dice sausage.*
Steam vegetables until tender. Bring water to a boil in small
saucepan. Add noodles and oil from packet, but do not add
seasoning packet. Drain noodles and add seasoning packet.
Stir well. Combine cooked sausage, steamed vegetables,
cooked noodles and ½ c. grated cheese. Place mixture in
casserole dish and sprinkle top with remaining ¼ c. cheese.
Warm casserole in oven until cheese is melted. (Another
method would be to leave casserole ingredients in covered
fying pan on stove top over medum heat until cheese is
melted.) Makes 3-5 servings.

*To eliminate some of the fat from link sausage, place the sau-
sage links in a skillet and add ½ cup of water. Cover and cook
slowly for 5 minutes. Remove lid and drain grease. Cook
slowly 12 to 15 minutes, turning with tongs until all sides
are brown. Cut into small pieces for the vegetable casserole.
Kitchen scissors work well.

Tip:

6 cooked shrimp, sautéed in
butter and minced garlic, or
2 c. cooked chicken, are also
very good in this recipe.

Baked Potato Bar

6 baked potatoes
1 lb. ground beef or ground turkey
½ c. chopped onion
4 sliced, fresh mushrooms
½ bag frozen broccoli
½ c. grated cheese
3 T. bacon pieces
1 tomato, diced
Ranch dressing, sour cream, or cottage cheese

Preheat oven to 400 degrees. Scrub potatoes well, prick with a fork, and bake for 1 hour-1 ¼ hours. Brown ground turkey and chopped onion in small amount of oil. (If ground beef is used you will not need the oil.) Add sliced mushrooms and fry them until tender. Steam broccoli. Top baked potatoes with the various toppings. Makes 5-6 servings.

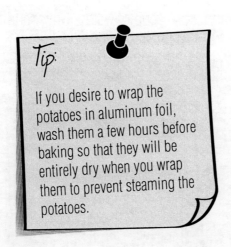

Tip:

If you desire to wrap the potatoes in aluminum foil, wash them a few hours before baking so that they will be entirely dry when you wrap them to prevent steaming the potatoes.

Chili Potato Topping

6 baked potatoes
1 lb. turkey burger
¼ c. green pepper, diced
28 oz. can diced tomatoes (do not drain)
15 oz. can pinto beans
¼ t. garlic powder
Sprinkle of cayenne pepper
1 t. cumin
½ t. oregano
½ t. pepper
½ t. salt

Brown the turkey burger and green pepper in oil. Add remaining ingredients. Bring to a boil and reduce heat. Simmer 30 minutes, stirring often. Spoon topping onto baked potatoes. Makes 5-6 servings.

*Another topping idea can be found at the bottom of P. 103.

Roast Beef

1 cross rib roast, chuck roast, sirloin tip roast
3-4 lbs. for a small roast; 5-6 lbs. for a large roast
1 T. minced, dried onion or 1 small onion, sliced
1 regular size oven bag
2 c. water for small roast; 4 c. water for large roast
Canola oil
Salt
Pepper
Garlic salt

Preheat oven to 325 degrees. Brown the roast in a deep, heavy pan with enough oil to cover the bottom of the pan. Open baking bag and place it in a 9" X 13" casserole dish. Do not place any flour in the bag as instructed by the bag manufacturer. Place roast in baking bag. Sprinkle the roast with seasonings and top with onions.

Pour water in the deep, heavy pan used to brown the roast. Stir to make a broth with the juices of the meat. Add broth to the seasoned roast inside of the baking bag. Close the baking bag with the tie provided and snip 3-4 small slits in the top of the bag.

Bake beef roast for 3-5 hours, depending on the size and cut of the roast. Makes 5-8 servings.

Gravy to Accompany Beef or Pork Roast

4 cups broth
4 T. cornstarch
6 T. cold water
Salt, pepper, lemon pepper, and garlic salt, to taste

To use broth from cooked roast, remove roast from baking bag to a plate. Keep roast warm in oven, if desired. Measure broth, and pour it through a strainer into a saucepan. Combine cornstarch and cold water. Thicken broth with corn starch and water by cooking over medium high heat until boiling thickens the gravy. Add additional water or thickening for desired smooth sauce. Season gravy to taste with seasonings.

Steak

2 tri-tip or top sirloin steak
Canola oil
Garlic salt
Pepper

Pour a light coating of oil on steak and spread it around with a spoon. Flip steaks over and repeat. Sprinkle well with garlic salt and pepper. Cook steak on grill using medium heat. Makes 2 servings.

Slow Cooked Roast

1 cross rib or chuck roast
1 T. gluten-free Worchestershire sauce
1 t. crushed garlic

Equivalency of onion soup mix:
1 T. gluten-free beef bouillon powder
2 T. instant minced dried onion
½ t. onion powder

Equivalency of 1 can cream of mushroom soup (P. 58)
(Most cream of mushroom/chicken soup has wheat in it.)

Preheat oven to 250 degrees. Cover the bottom and sides of a 9" X 13" casserole dish with a piece of aluminum foil. Place roast on foil. Mix remaining ingredients and pour over roast. Cover roast with a piece of aluminum foil. Fold over edges of the two pieces of foil together and seal. Bake roast for 8-9 hours. Use broth mixture for gravy. Makes 5-8 servings.

Steak (or Chicken) Fajitas

If possible, prepare this marinade the night before, and marinate meat overnight.

Combine the following ingredients for marinade:

2 T. lime juice
2 T. canola or olive oil
½ c. chopped fresh cilantro
¼ c. gluten-free soy sauce
1 t. gluten-free Worcestershire sauce
4 cloves minced garlic
1 t. dried oregano leaves
1 t. cumin
3 medium-sized steaks (or 4 boneless chicken breasts)

Slice steak (or chicken) into thin strips. Pour marinade over strips of meat and marinate overnight in covered bowl or sealable bag. Remove meat to a separate bowl, reserving marinade.

½ green bell pepper
½ red bell pepper
½ yellow bell pepper
½ large onion
6-8 corn tortillas
Refried beans
Tomatoes, chopped
Cilantro, chopped
Salsa
Guacamole
Sour cream

(Continued on next page)

Steak (or Chicken) Fajitas, Continued

Slice green, red and yellow peppers. Slice onion. Pour enough of the reserved marinade to cover the bottom of a non-stick pan. Add vegetables and cook over medium heat until tender crisp. Remove to platter and keep warm. Add marinade to cover bottom of frying pan and add beef or chicken strips. Stir fry meat until done. Combine cooked vegetables and meat. Serve with warm tortillas, refried beans, chopped tomatoes, chopped cilantro, salsa, guacamole and sour cream. Makes 5-7 servings.

Guacamole

1 large avocado, mashed
½ c. gluten-free mayonnaise
¼ t. lemon juice
3 T. salsa
Garlic salt, to taste

Peel avocado and remove pit. Mash with fork and add remaining ingredients. Stir well.

Tip:

This guacamole recipe is wonderful as a dip for potato chips.

Shepherd's Pie

1 ½ lbs. ground beef or turkey burger
Garlic salt to taste
3 T. oil
½ c. chopped onion
¼ t. salt
⅛ t. pepper
2 cans green beans, drained
2 - 8 oz. cans tomato sauce
2 c. mashed potatoes
Grated cheese, if tolerated

Cook hamburger (or turkey burger and oil), pepper, and onion. Add green beans and tomato sauce. Place in a 9" X 13" casserole dish with mashed potatoes and cheese on top. Bake at 350 degrees for 30 minutes, or until cheese melts. Makes 6-8 servings.

Lasagna

1 pkg. gluten-free lasagna noodles
1 t. crushed garlic
1 lb. ground beef
3 ½ c. gluten-free spaghetti sauce
1 ¾ c. cottage cheese
2 c. grated Italian blend cheese
¼ c. sour cream
Grated Parmesan cheese

Preheat oven to 350 degrees. Cook noodles. While noodles are cooking, brown ground beef and add crushed garlic and spaghetti sauce. Simmer for 4-5 minutes. Coat some of the sauce mixture thinly over bottom of a 9" x 13" baking dish. Place one-third of cooked gluten-free noodles over sauce. Combine cottage cheese, 1 c. of the grated cheese, and sour cream. Divide amount in half and spread evenly over noodles. Place another layer of gluten-free noodles. Add half of remaining sauce and spread evenly over noodles.

Repeat with remainder of cottage cheese mixture. Place another layer of gluten-free noodles. Add sauce. Top with reserved 1 c. of grated cheese. Sprinkle well with Parmesan cheese. Cover lasagna and bake for 30-40 minutes, or until cheese melts and lasagna is heated throughout. Makes 8-10 servings.

BBQ Meatballs

Meatballs:

1 lb. ground beef
1 egg
1 small onion, diced
¾ c. gluten-free bread crumbs
1 T. gluten-free Worcestershire sauce
1 clove minced garlic
1 t. salt
1 t. pepper

BBQ Sauce:

1 ½ T. gluten-free Worcestershire Sauce
¾ c. grape jelly
1 ½ c. ketchup
3 T. mustard
1 clove minced garlic

Preheat oven to 400 degrees. Mix meatball ingredients and form into balls. Place in 9" x 13" baking dish or jelly roll cookie sheet and pour BBQ Sauce or Sweet and Sour Sauce (see next page) on the meatballs. Bake uncovered for 20 to 25 minutes. Cooked meatballs should be firm. Makes 5-7 servings.

Sweet and Sour Meatballs

Use directions to make meatballs as found on previous page.

This recipe amount is large and allows for extra sauce to serve over rice as a side dish with the meatballs. If no extra sauce is needed, cut recipe in half.

Sweet and Sour Sauce:

1 ½ c. sugar
4 T. cornstarch
4 T. ketchup
1 T. vinegar
1 c. pineapple juice
½ c. water
2 T. lemon juice
Cooked rice

Combine and boil until thick. Pour over meatballs and cooked rice.

*This sauce is also excellent on cooked chicken strips and fried rice.

Chili

2 small cans stewed tomatoes, blended
2 small cans of gluten-free chili
1 lb. ground beef, cooked
1 onion, diced
1 can kidney beans, drained
1 can black beans, drained
Chili powder to taste

Simmer in slow cooker on low for 6-8 hours. Makes 7-9 servings.

Another Chili Recipe

2 lbs. extra lean ground beef
1 onion, sliced
4 cans gluten-free pork and beans
1 can pinto beans
1 can kidney beans
1 small can diced tomatoes
1 ½ T. chili powder
2 c. salsa
Garlic salt, to taste
Pepper, to taste

Fry ground beef and onion until completely cooked. Drain and rinse pinto beans and kidney beans. Combine all ingredients together in a large pot. Bring to a gentle boil, then turn heat down and allow chili to simmer for 1 ½ hours. Makes 8-10 servings.

Chili Relleno Casserole

2 cans whole green chilies, drained
8 oz. Monterey Jack cheese, sliced in strips
4 eggs
1 ½ T. milk
3 ½ T. rice flour
¼ t. salt
¼ t. crushed garlic
1 c. grated cheddar cheese

Preheat oven to 350 degrees. Grease 9" X13" baking dish. Place the green chilies in a single layer in baking dish and cover green chilies with cheese strips. Separate the egg whites and yolks into two mixing bowls. Whip egg whites first at high speed until they hold high peaks. Add the milk, rice flour, salt, and crushed garlic to the egg yolks in the other bowl and beat until smooth. Fold egg yolk mixture into beaten egg whites and spread over the chilies. Quickly top with grated cheddar cheese and bake for 16-20 minutes. Makes 6-8 servings.

Beef Stroganoff

Prepared gluten-free noodles or rice
1 pound beef sirloin steak (or leftover roast beef)
1 T. rice flour
½ t. salt
2 T. butter
1 ½ c. sliced fresh mushrooms
½ c. diced onion
1 clove garlic, minced

Slice meat into thin strips while partially frozen, across the grain of the meat. Combine rice flour and salt; coat meat with mixture. In a skillet, heat butter, add meat, and brown quickly on both sides. Add mushrooms, onion, and garlic. Cook until onions are tender. Remove meat/vegetable mixture from the pan and set aside. Reserve drippings in pan.

Stroganoff Sauce:

2 T. butter
2 T. rice flour
1 t. gluten-free instant beef bouillon granules or powder
¼ t. salt
1 ¼ c. water
½ c. sour cream
1 T. additional rice flour

On medium high heat, add butter and rice flour to pan drippings in skillet. Add bouillon, salt, and water. Stir constantly with a whisk until mixture simmers and thickens. Add meat mixture back into skillet. Combine sour cream and rice flour, and add to meat mixture. Heat through, but do not boil. Serve over cooked gluten-free elbow or fettucine noodles, or rice. Makes 5-7 servings.

Ground Beef Gravy with Potatoes

6-7 baked potatoes
1 lb. ground beef
3 c. water
1 T. gluten-free powdered beef bouillon
3 T. cornstarch

Prepare baked potatoes. Brown the ground beef until cooked. Remove ground beef to a bowl, leaving bits of ground beef in the frying pan. Combine water, bouillon, and cornstarch in a bowl until well mixed. Add to frying pan and bring to a boil. Stir constantly and reduce heat to medium. Cook until thickened.

Beef Enchiladas

1 lb. ground beef
1 doz. gluten-free corn tortillas
1 can refried beans
1 chopped onion
Gluten-free enchilada sauce (or use recipe below)
2 c. grated cheese
Sour cream
Shredded lettuce
Chopped tomatoes

Preheat oven to 350 degrees. Brown ground beef. Microwave tortillas in slightly moist paper towels until pliable. Mix refried beans and cooked ground beef in frying pan and heat until warm. Place beans and hamburger in tortilla and roll the tortilla. Line up rolled tortillas in a greased 9" X 13" casserole dish. Cover tortillas with canned (or homemade) sauce and cheese. Bake for 35-45 minutes. Top enchiladas with sour cream, lettuce, and tomatoes. Makes 6-8 servings.

Beef Enchilada Sauce

2 c. water
⅛ c. cornstarch
½ T. chili powder
1 t. onion powder
½ t. garlic powder
1 T. gluten-free beef bouillon
⅛ t. oregano leaves
¼ c. canola oil
¼ t. salt
½ T. sugar
¼ t. cumin

Combine all in a saucepan and boil for 1 minute.

Green Chili Tacos

1 lb. ground beef
1 t. crushed garlic
1 small onion, diced
1 small can green chilies
1 tomato, chopped
1 ¼ cup grated cheddar cheese
12 gluten-free taco shells
2 c. lettuce, shredded
1 fresh tomato, chopped
1 small onion, diced, raw
Salsa, fresh or bottled
Ranch dressing

Brown the ground beef with garlic and onion. Drain any fat.
Add green chilies, tomato, and cheese. Simmer, stirring often,
until well blended.

Put meat mixture into hard taco shells or warmed corn tortillas
and serve with lettuce and fresh chopped tomatoes, onions,
ranch dressing, and salsa. Makes 4-6 servings.

Tacos

1 1b. cooked ground beef or chicken
Gluten-free taco seasoning mix or Mexican seasoning, to
taste
2 c. lettuce, shredded
2 c. grated cheese
¼ c. onions, diced
½ c. diced tomatoes
12 gluten-free corn tortillas or corn shells
Sour cream or ranch dressing
Salsa

Cook ground beef or chicken in a skillet. Sprinkle with taco seasoning mix or Mexican seasoning. Prepare vegetables and other toppings. Warm tortillas in a slightly moist paper towel (or clean dish towel) in the microwave until heated through and soft. Serve tacos with gluten-free sour cream or ranch dressing and gluten-free salsa. Makes 5-7 servings.

Meatloaf

1 lb. ground beef
1 egg, slightly beaten
½ c. gluten-free bread or gluten-free cracker crumbs
½ c. diced onion
1 clove garlic, minced
1 T. ketchup
1 T. horseradish
1 ½ t. salt
1 t. sugar
⅔ c. milk

Preheat oven to 350 degrees. Combine egg with ground beef. Add remaining ingredients and mix well. Press into a loaf pan. Spread additional ketchup on top, if desired. Cover with foil and bake for 1 hour. Makes 5-7 servings.

Bacon Ranch Hamburgers

4 hamburger patties
4 Kinnikinnick® Gluten-free Hamburger Buns (or gluten-free
bread)
8 slices bacon
1 large tomato, sliced
4 lettuce leaves
Ranch dressing

Fry or grill hamburger patties and fry bacon until completely done.   Microwave or toast gluten-free hamburger buns. Slice tomato and wash lettuce leaves. Serve hamburgers topped with 2 slices of bacon, tomato, lettuce, and ranch dressing. Makes 4 servings.

Spaghetti

1 pkg. gluten-free spaghetti noodles
½ lb. ground beef
3 c. gluten-free spaghetti sauce
Garlic salt, to taste
Onion salt, to taste
¼ c. Parmesan cheese

Cook noodles. Cook ground beef until browned. Combine with sauce, and season with garlic and onion salt. Simmer for 15 min. while cooking the noodles. Drain and rinse the spaghetti. Serve with Parmesan cheese sprinkled across the top.   Makes 8 servings.

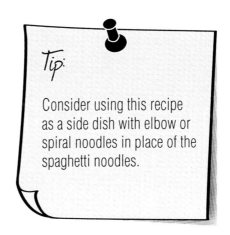

Tip:

Consider using this recipe as a side dish with elbow or spiral noodles in place of the spaghetti noodles.

Tortilla Wrap Ideas

Surround the gluten-free corn tortillas in a moist paper towel or wrap them in a clean dish towel. Place them in the microwave until they are soft and pliable, approximately 2 minutes for 12 tortillas. Tortillas may also be warmed by frying them in hot oil. Instructions for making a tortilla pouch for warming tortillas in the microwave may be found online by searching for "microwave potato bag."

Pizza Tortillas: Top a tortilla with spaghetti sauce, pepperoni, cheese, and other desired toppings. Put another tortilla on top and fry in small amount of oil on both sides until lightly browned and cheese is melted. Cut into pie-shaped pieces and serve warm.

Spanish Wrap: Top a fried or microwaved tortilla with a scoop of refried beans, and add lettuce, shredded cheese, chopped tomatoes, and a mixture of ranch dressing and salsa.

Tuna Wrap: Top a microwaved tortilla with a mixture of tuna and mayonnaise, a pickle spear, and lettuce.

Scrambled Egg Wrap: Top a fried or microwaved tortilla with scrambled eggs, bacon pieces, mayonnaise, and shredded cheese.

Hard Cooked Egg Wrap: Top a microwaved tortilla with hard cooked eggs mixed with mayonnaise, lettuce, and pickle relish or dill pickle spear.

Lunch Meat Wrap: Top a microwaved tortilla with mayonnaise and a piece of gluten-free lunch meat. Add lettuce, chopped tomatoes, and a pickle spear.

Chicken Wrap: Top a tortilla with gluten-free chicken chunks combined with mayonnaise, avocado spears, shredded lettuce, bacon pieces, and lemon pepper.

Chili Wrap: Top a fried or microwaved tortilla with gluten-free chili, shredded cheese, lettuce, and ranch dressing.

Cinnamon Sugar Wrap: Spread microwaved tortilla with butter and cinnamon sugar. Roll tortilla and slice it into one inch pieces. Secure with toothpick, if desired.

More Tortilla Wrap Ideas

Roast Beef Wrap

½ c. cooked roast beef
2 c. gravy
1 - 4 oz. can mild green chilies
1 T. sour cream
6 tortillas, warmed
Grated cheese

Chop roast into small pieces. Place meat, gravy, and green chiles in a frying pan and heat until warm. Warm tortillas in the microwave, or fry them in hot oil until soft. Make a line of meat/gravy mixture down the middle of each tortilla. Sprinkle with grated cheese. Roll tortillas and serve. Makes 4-6 servings.

Sloppy Joe Wrap

1 lb. ground beef
½ c. onion, chopped or 1 T. minced dried onion
¼ c. celery, chopped
1 - 8 oz. can tomato sauce
1 ½ t. gluten-free Worchestershire sauce
¼ c. ketchup
1 t. apple cider vinegar
1 T. sugar
½ t. salt
½ t. pepper
½ t. crushed garlic

Brown the ground beef with onions and celery. Add remaining ingredients and simmer until vegetables are tender. Serve on warmed corn tortillas. Makes 4-6 servings.

Pizza

2 t. yeast
½ c. lukewarm water
2 t. sugar
1 ¼ c. warm milk or soy milk
2 c. rice flour
1 ½ c. tapioca flour
2 ½ t. xanthan gum
½ c. dried potato flakes
1 t. salt
1 ½ t. Italian Seasoning
¼ c. shortening
2 T. butter

Preheat oven to 400 degrees. Pour warm water into a small bowl, and sprinkle yeast and sugar across the top of the water. Microwave the milk until warm. Combine dry ingredients in a large bowl, preferably a heavy duty kitchen mixer. Mix yeast mixture, warm milk, shortening, and butter into dry ingredients. Beat at high speed for 3 min. Spray or grease pizza pans. Press dough onto pizza pans until very thin by placing a clean sandwich or bread bag on your hand and press dough onto two greased, large, round pizza pans. Bake 10 minutes on middle shelf of oven. Add sauce, pepperoni, Canadian bacon, cheese (or non-dairy substitute), etc., and bake another 10-20 minutes until bottom of crust is lightly browned. Makes 2 large pizzas (9-14 servings).

Alfredo Pizza

*Prepare Alfredo sauce at least a half hour ahead to allow time for sauce to thicken before beginning pizza.

4 oz. cream cheese
⅛ c. butter
¼ c. Parmesan cheese
1 c. milk
¼ t. garlic powder
¼ t. pepper
5 pieces bacon, fried
2 chicken breasts, fried or grilled
1/ 4 t. seasoned salt
1 c. grated cheese

Combine cream cheese, butter, Parmesan cheese, milk, garlic powder, and pepper in medium saucepan and cook until smooth and warm. Refrigerate for 1/2 hour or more. Preheat oven to 400 degrees. Use crust recipe on previous page. Bake crust in oven for 10 minutes. Cook bacon and chicken and cut into small pieces. Add seasoned salt to chicken and stir well. Spread sauce over two large pizza crusts. Sprinkle cooked bacon, cooked chicken, and grated cheese over pizza. Bake for approximately 10 minutes. Makes 2 pizzas (9-14 servings).

Breadsticks

Preheat oven to 400 degrees. Use the roll recipe on P. 32, but add 2 t. Italian seasoning. Scoop dough into a large plastic freezer bag. Cut a ½" opening diagonally on one corner of the bag. Holding the bag upright, squeeze each line of dough out onto greased cookie sheet. Sprinkle breadsticks lightly with garlic salt and Parmesan cheese. Bake breadsticks for 14-18 minutes. Makes 6-8 servings.

Fried Fish

5 pieces snow cod or pollock fish
¼ c. brown rice flour
¼ c. corn flour
Canola oil
Garlic salt, to taste
Lemon pepper, to taste

Combine brown rice flour and corn flour in a pie plate and dip fish on both sides in flour mixture. Place fish in a non-stick frying pan or on a griddle, coated with oil. Sprinkle both sides of fish with garlic salt and lemon pepper. Fry until golden brown and cooked throughout. Makes 5 servings.

Grilled Salmon

2 t. olive or canola oil
2 t. fresh lemon juice
½ t. salt
2 cloves garlic, minced, or 1 ½ t. crushed garlic
1 t. thyme leaves
½ t. lemon pepper
3 pieces salmon or about 1 lb.

Combine all ingredients except salmon in a gallon size plastic freezer bag. Squeeze bag until ingredients are mixed. Add salmon and coat well with mixture. Remove salmon from bag and place on broiler pan sprayed with cooking spray. Broil until salmon is cooked throughout, approximately 6-10 minutes. Makes 5-6 servings.

Ralph, age 45

In thinking back on my childhood, frequent indigestion and heartburn were a common occurance. I would try changing the types of foods I was eating, but it didn't seem to make that much difference in how I felt. A few years ago I started having chest pain and nausea on a frequent basis. I would start feeling weak like I needed to eat, but I didn't want to eat because I would feel sick to my stomach, and the chest pain would become worse.

I had an endoscopy done, and it showed that bile was backwashing into my stomach and causing significant irritation; it also showed moderate to severe inflammation in the esophagus. My doctor prescribed a medicine to reduce acid, and I began taking double doses of the medicine to help with my symptoms. The chest pain gradually went away and my symptoms were lessened, but I still had some difficulty.

Around this time my mother was diagnosed with celiac disease. I eventually made a real effort to cut gluten out of my diet entirely. Within about 2 weeks I began to notice improvement and then it became easy to stay on the diet. My appetite improved and I began to look forward to eating, knowing that I didn't have to worry about how I would feel afterwards. The food seemed to taste better as well. I also noticed that I didn't seem to need my heartburn medicine as much, so I stopped taking it.

I tried the diet for 2 years and stayed off my medicine, and then I had another endoscopy done and the results were very encouraging. I didn't have any more problems with the bile backing up into my stomach and my esophagus was back to normal. I attribute my improvement to following a gluten-free diet.

Desserts and Drinks

Pretzel Cereal Snack

3 T. honey
2 T. butter
3 T. peanut butter
2 c. Health Valley® Rice Crunch 'Ems
2 c. EnviroKidz® Gorilla Munch
1 pkg. Ener-G® Foods Crisp (wheat free) Pretzels
⅓ c. peanuts (optional)

Preheat oven to 175 degrees. Combine honey, butter, and peanut butter and heat in microwave for around 1 minute or less, until mixture is smooth. Pour over combined cereal, pretzels, and peanuts. Spread on baking sheet and bake for 1- 1 ½ hours. Makes 4-6 servings.

Peanut Butter Cereal Bars

1 c. corn syrup
1 c. sugar
1 ¼ c. creamy peanut butter
3 c. Post® Cocoa Pebbles
4 ½ c. Health Valley® Rice Crunch 'Ems

Heat corn syrup, sugar, and peanut butter and mix together until consistency is smooth and sugar dissolves. Add cereal and stir well. Press into greased 9" X 13" casserole dish. Makes 9-12 servings.

Another Cereal Bar Recipe

2 cubes butter
1 ½ c. light corn syrup
1 ½ c. sugar
12 oz. box Rice Chex® or Health Valley® Rice Crunch 'Ems
¾ t. baking soda
2 t. vanilla
½ c. coconut
1 c. almond slivers

Boil butter, corn syrup, and sugar until it reaches the soft ball stage on a candy thermometer. Remove from stove burner and add soda and vanilla. Mix well and add cereal, coconut, and almonds. Stir well. Press into greased 9" X 13" casserole dish. Makes 9-12 servings.

Corn Flake Treats

1 c. sugar
1 c. corn syrup
½ t. salt
½ t. vanilla
1 c. peanut butter
8 c. gluten-free corn flakes or EnviroKidz® Amazon Frosted
Flakes

Stir and boil sugar and corn syrup until sugar is dissolved.
(Do not boil too long, or end result is a very firm treat.) Add
remaining ingredients and stir well. Press into greased 9" X
13" casserole dish and wait until treats are firm before serving.
Makes 9-12 servings.

Rice Cake Candy Bars

¼ c. honey or sugar
⅓ c. almond or peanut butter
1 T. cocoa or carob powder
1-2 T. very hot water
⅓ c. slivered almonds
⅓ c. sunflower seeds
1 c. brown rice cakes, broken into small pieces

Chop almonds and sunflower seeds in blender. Set aside. Heat sugar and peanut butter, and add cocoa. Add hot water, and then add almonds and sunflower seeds. Take off heat and add broken rice cakes. Form into bars on pieces of tinfoil. Wrap up and refrigerate or freeze. Makes 2-4 servings.

Marshmallow Treats

⅓ c. butter
½ pkg. marshmallows
6 - 6 ½ c. Post® Cocoa Pebbles®, Post® Fruity Pebbles®,
Health Valley® Rice Crunch 'Ems®, or EnviroKidz® Gorilla
Munch® Cereal, or a mix

Melt butter and ½ package marshmallows (36 large marshmallows) in a large saucepan over medium heat. Add cereal and stir well. Press into greased 9" X 13" casserole dish. Makes 9-12 servings.

Caramel Corn

6 quarts popped popcorn

½ c. butter
¼ c. light corn syrup
1 c. brown sugar
1 t. salt

Bring butter, corn syrup, brown sugar, and salt to a rolling boil for 1 minute. Remove from heat. Pour over popcorn and stir. Makes 8-10 servings.

Corn Chip Candy

1 c. peanut butter
1 c. light corn syrup
¾ c. sugar
1 bag of Fritos®

Pour corn chips into a large bowl. Heat peanut butter, corn syrup, and sugar until it comes to a boil. Quickly remove from heat and pour over one regular sized bag of corn chips. Stir well. Makes 8-10 servings.

Hard Candy

2 c. sugar
1 c. water
⅔ c. corn syrup
1 t. flavoring, like cinnamon, root beer extract, or lemon

Boil for around 25-30 min. until mixture reaches 300 degrees on a candy thermometer. Add flavoring. Pour into greased jelly roll cookie sheet or molds. Use caution. Mixture will be extremely hot. Makes 8-10 servings.

Peanut Butter Heaven

1 c. sugar
1 c. light corn syrup
1 c. peanut butter
4 c. gluten-free EnviroKidz® Koala Crisp® Cereal
½ c. milk chocolate chips
½ c. butterscotch chips

Bring sugar and corn syrup to a boil. (Do not boil very long or this dessert will harden too much.) Add peanut butter and mix well. Add cereal and stir until combined. Spray a 9" x 13" casserole dish with cooking spray. Scoop mixture into dish and press down until mixture is level. Melt chocolate and butterscotch chips in microwave, taking care to watch them carefully so they don't burn. Spread over cereal mixture. Refrigerate until ready to serve. Makes 9-12 servings.

Cinnamon Sugar Cookies

½ c. butter, softened
1 c. sugar
1 egg
1 t. vanilla
1 ⅓ c. brown rice flour
⅔ c. tapioca flour
½ c. sorghum flour
½ t. baking soda
¼ t. salt
1 t. xanthan gum
¼ c. water

Cream butter, sugar, egg, and vanilla. Add dry ingredients and water. Mix until combined.

3 T. brown sugar
1 ½ T. cinnamon sugar

Preheat oven to 350 degrees. Combine brown sugar and cinnamon sugar. Dip spoonful of cookie dough into mixture of brown sugar and cinnamon. Place ball of dough on greased cookie sheet. Bake cookies for 11-13 minutes. Makes 24 cookies.

*The best results come when the amount of dough used for each cookie is slightly larger than a whole walnut. Gluten-free cookie dough spreads more than other dough. For best results let the cookies set for a few minutes before removing them from the cookie sheet.

Applesauce Cookies

½ c. shortening
1 c. sugar
1 egg
1 t. vanilla
1 c. applesauce
1 c. brown rice flour
½ c. potato starch
½ c. tapioca flour
1 t. baking powder
1 ½ t. xanthan gum
1 t. baking soda
½ t. salt
½ t. ground cinnamon
⅛ t. ground nutmeg
¼ t. ground cloves

Preheat oven to 350 degrees. Cream first five ingredients. Add dry ingredients and mix until combined. Spray cookie sheet with cooking spray. Drop batter by small spoonfuls onto cookie sheet. Bake for 11-13 minutes. Makes 32 cookies.

*For best results let the cookies set for a few minutes before removing them from the cookie sheet.

Sugar Cookies

1 c. sugar
¾ c. butter
1 egg
1 T. sour cream
1 T. vanilla
1 c. brown rice flour
⅓ c. potato starch
⅓ c. tapioca flour
⅛ c. sorghum flour
2 T. corn flour
1 t. baking powder
2 t. xanthan gum

Cream sugar, butter, egg, sour cream, and vanilla together. Add dry ingredients and mix until combined. Do not overmix. Divide dough into 2 sections and place each section of dough onto plastic wrap. Form each section of dough into a log shape. (The log shape cannot be made too easily yet, because the dough is too soft at this point.) Place in fridge for at least one hour. Preheat oven to 350 degrees. Remove dough from fridge and roll again into a log shape, with about 1 ½ inch diameter. If dough stays in the log shape and is easy to slice, begin cutting dough into ¼" slices. If not, return dough to fridge until firm. Spray cookie sheet with cooking spray. Place sliced cookie dough on cookie sheet. Bake for 11-13 minutes. Makes 48 small cookies.

No Bake Cookies

2 c. sugar
½ c. milk
1 cube butter
5 T. cocoa
3 c. gluten-free oats* (be sure these were grown separately from wheat)
1 t. vanilla

Combine first four ingredients and boil for 1 minute in saucepan. Add oats. Simmer for 5 minutes (while stirring constantly) to soften oats. Add vanilla. Scoop out mixture using a 1/4 c. measure onto wax paper. Allow to become firm before eating. Makes 13-14 cookies.

*Some people with celiac disease cannot tolerate gluten-free oatmeal. Please check with your physician before adding oatmeal to your diet.

Chocolate Chip Cookies

Combine:
1 c. butter
¾ c. sugar
¾ c. brown sugar
1 t. vanilla
2 eggs

Add and mix:
½ c. sorghum flour
2 c. brown rice flour
¾ c. tapioca flour
1 t. xanthan gum
1 t. baking soda
1 t. salt
1 ½ c. chocolate chips (If milk intolerant, use Enjoy Life®
Chocolate Chips)

Bake at 375 degrees for 10-11 minutes on a greased cookie sheet. Makes 36 cookies.

*The best results come when the amount of dough used for each cookie is slightly larger than a whole walnut. Gluten-free cookie dough spreads more than other dough. For best results let the cookies set for a few minutes before removing them from the cookie sheet.

Butterscotch Cookies

Substitute the following for the chocolate chips:

¾ c. butterscotch chips
⅔ c. toffee bits

Peanut Butter Cookies

1 c. sugar
1 t. baking soda
1 c. creamy peanut butter
1 large egg
½ t. vanilla

Preheat oven to 350 degrees. Mix sugar and baking soda. Add remaining ingredients and mix thoroughly. Chill for 30 minutes in fridge or 10 minutes in freezer. Shape into small balls of dough (about 1 T. each) and place on greased cookie sheet. Bake for 10 minutes. Makes 27 cookies.

Chewy Chocolate Cookies

1 ¼ c. butter
2 c. sugar
2 eggs
2 t. vanilla
1 c. brown rice flour
⅔ c. tapioca flour
⅓ c. sorghum flour
1 t. xanthan gum
1 t. soda
¾ t. salt
¾ c. cocoa

Preheat oven to 350 degrees. Combine first four ingredients until creamy. Add dry ingredients and mix until combined. Drop by spoonful on greased cookie sheet and bake for 9-11 minutes. Makes 44 cookies.

*The best results come when the amount of dough used for each cookie is slightly larger than a whole walnut. Gluten-free cookie dough spreads more than other dough. For best results let the cookies set for a few minutes before removing them from the cookie sheet.

Best Toffee

2 ⅓ c. chopped almonds
2 - 7 oz. grated chocolate bars
1 1b. butter
2 ½ c. sugar
⅓ c. almonds
2 T. light corn syrup
1 c. water

Prepare almonds and chocolate before starting to cook the re-maining toffee ingredients. Chop almonds and separate them into three measured amounts: 1 c. for bottom of toffee, 1 c. for top of toffee, and ⅓ c. in toffee. Grate one candy bar at a time and place shavings in separate bowls.

Spread 1 c. almonds and sprinkle shavings from one candy bar onto cookie sheet. Combine last five ingredients in heavy saucepan. Bring ingredients to a boil on medium high heat, stirring constantly until mixture reaches 285 degrees and color changes to a medium tan. Pour mixture onto almonds and chocolate by pouring from the center outward. Sprinkle re-maining almonds and chocolate over hot toffee and press them into toffee with a drinking glass. Allow toffee to set up for 5 hours at room temperature. Makes 15-20 servings.

Tips:

-You can turn the heat up, but don't turn it down.
-Leave a metal spoon with a heat-proof handle in the toffee. If you remove it, get another clean spoon. This reduces the chance of toffee having sugar crystals.
-Don't speed the cooling of the toffee.

Chocolate Surprise

1st Layer: Graham Cracker Crust (see P. 179)

2nd Layer: 1 c. powdered sugar
8 oz. cream cheese
1 c. whipped topping from 12 oz. container

3rd Layer: 1 large box chocolate pudding (not instant)
1 small box chocolate pudding (not instant)
Milk (see pudding directions)

4th Layer: Remainder of 12 oz. whipped topping
(1 c. was used in Layer 2)

Make graham cracker crust and press crust into 9" x 13" casserole dish. Cool crust completely. Cream together powdered sugar and cream cheese. Fold in whipped topping. Smooth mixture onto top of crust and place in fridge while preparing next layer. Prepare pudding and allow it to cool slightly. Pour over cream cheese layer. When pudding has completely cooled, add whipped topping by the spoonful and carefully smooth it over the pudding. Refrigerate at least two hours. Makes 9-12 servings.

Variation: Add ¼ c. creamy peanut butter to pudding.

Rice Pudding

1 T. butter
4 c. half and half cream, or soy milk, or almond milk
1 ¼ c. cooked rice
¼ t. salt
½ c. honey
4 slightly beaten eggs
¼ t. vanilla
½ t. lemon extract
Nutmeg

Preheat oven to 300 degrees. Grease 1 1/2 qt. glass baking dish with butter. Combine all ingredients, except nutmeg, and pour into baking dish. Sprinkle top of mixture with nutmeg. Bake uncovered for 35-45 minutes. It will start to gel when it is done. Turn oven off and leave pudding in oven for 10 minutes. Makes 6-8 servings.

Apple Crisp

2 quarts gluten-free canned apple pie filling
¾ c. brown sugar
¼ c. brown rice flour
¼ c. tapioca flour
½ c. crumbled salted rice cakes or gluten-free oatmeal
¾ t. cinnamon
⅓ c. soft butter

Preheat oven to 375 degrees. Pour apple pie filling into 9" X 13" casserole dish. Combine dry ingredients in medium bowl and cut butter in. Sprinkle mixture over top of pie filling. Bake for 40-45 minutes. Makes 9-12 servings.

*Some people with celiac disease cannot tolerate gluten-free oatmeal. Please check with your physician before adding oatmeal to your diet.

Fudge

2 c. sugar
⅔ c. evaporated milk or soymilk
2 T. butter
Dash of salt
1 ½ c. milk chocolate chips
2 ½ c. mini marshmallows
2 t. vanilla

Combine first four ingredients and boil for 5 minutes in saucepan. Remove from heat and add chocolate chips and marshmallows. Stir until chocolate and marshmallows are melted. Add vanilla and stir well. Spray an 8" X 8" casserole or baking dish with cooking spray. Spread fudge into dish. Cool completely in fridge before serving. Makes 9 servings.

Another Fudge Recipe: Rocky Road Style

4 ½ c. sugar
1 can evaporated milk
2 cubes butter
2 c. milk chocolate chips
1 large bag miniature marshmallows
3 - 7 oz. milk chocolate bars, frozen
2 T. vanilla

Boil first three ingredients. Reduce heat and cook for 10 minutes. Remove from heat and add remaining ingredients. Stir until smooth. Marshmallows will not melt if using frozen candy bars. Spray a 9" X 13" casserole dish with cooking spray. Spread fudge into dish. Cool completely in fridge before serving. Makes 12-15 servings.

Graham Cracker Crust

2 T. brown sugar
⅓ c. sugar
1 c. brown rice flour
⅓ c. tapioca flour
⅛ c. potato starch
⅛ c. sorghum flour
¼ t. salt
½ t. xanthan gum
1 t. baking powder
½ t. baking soda
¼ c. softened butter
2 t. vanilla
2 T. water
¼ c. canola oil

Preheat oven to 325 degrees. Combine dry ingredients. Use pastry blender, two knives, or heavy duty kitchen mixer to cut in softened butter, vanilla, water, and oil. Spoon crumbs into pie plate. Press crumbs evenly across the bottom and sides of the pie plate. Bake for 20-23 minutes for pie crust or 24-26 minutes for 9" X 13" (for a dessert recipe). Makes two pie crusts or one 9" X 13".

Pie Crust

¾ c. white rice flour or brown rice flour
½ c. potato starch
¾ c. tapioca flour
¼ c. sorghum flour
¼ c. corn flour (or masa, found in Mexican food section)
½ t. salt
1 t. baking powder
1 t. xanthan gum
1 T. sugar
¾ c. shortening
1 egg, beaten
½ c. cold water per pie crust, as needed
¾ t. apple cider vinegar

Sift dry ingredients into a large bowl. Add shortening and cut it into the dry ingredients with a pastry cutter, two table knives, or heavy duty kitchen mixer. In a small bowl beat eggs, water, and vinegar. Add mixture to the dry ingredients and mix well. Divide the pastry dough into 2-3 equal parts. Wrap extra pie crust dough in plastic wrap and place them in a heavy plastic bag in the freezer.

Spread pie crust thinly into pie plate using a clean plastic bag over your hand. Another method is to spread a large piece of plastic film on kitchen counter and place one piece of dough there. Cover with a second piece of film and roll out the dough within the two pieces of plastic film. If pastry dough seems sticky and hard to remove from the plastic, pat rice flour over the surface. If it cracks and seems dry, add 1 1/2 t. water. Remove the top piece of plastic film, laying the rolled dough into your pie plate, and removing the bottom piece of plastic film. Prick pie crust with a fork. For a pre-baked crust, bake at 400 degrees for 10-15 minutes. Makes 2-3 pie crusts.

Cream Pie Filling

Pie crust
1 c. sugar
¼ c. cornstarch or potato starch
¼ t. salt
3 c. milk
2 eggs
3 T. butter
1 ½ t. vanilla
1 baked pie shell
2 sliced bananas or ½ c. shredded coconut

Prepare a gluten-free pie crust or gluten-free graham cracker crust. In a medium saucepan, combine sugar, cornstarch, salt, and milk. Cook and stir over medium heat until thickened and bubbly. Reduce heat; cook and stir 2 minutes more. Remove from heat. Beat eggs in a small bowl. Gradually stir in 1 cup of the hot mixture into the eggs. Slowly pour egg mixture into saucepan while stirring and bring mixture to a gentle boil. Cook and stir for 2 minutes more. Remove from heat and add butter and vanilla. Slice bananas and spread across bottom of pie shell. Pour cream filling over baked pie shell with bananas. Or add coconut to the cream filling and sprinkle coconut across the top of the pie for a coconut cream pie. Makes 6-8 servings.

Apple Pie

1-2 quarts gluten-free apple pie filling*
Gluten-free pie crust for bottom and top of pie

Preheat oven to 350 degrees. Place bottom pie crust on pie plate, covering sides and bottom and allowing ¾ inch of extra pie crust on outer top edge. Pour pie filling into uncooked crust. (The amount of pie filling may vary due to the size of the pie plate.) Cover with top pie crust. Fold extra 1 inch from bottom pie crust over top crust and seal. Flute edge of crust. Cut an apple shape (or slits) into top crust for venting of steam. Bake for 50-60 minutes, or until crust is golden brown. Makes 6-8 servings.

*The recipe for canned Apple Pie Filling (see P. 215) can also be used. Reduce recipe for around 6-7 c. of apples per pie.

Peach Pie

2 gluten-free pie crusts
1 c. sugar
1 c. water
3 T. cornstarch or potato starch
¼ c. butter
⅛ t. salt
½ t. vanilla or almond flavoring
6-8 c. fresh peaches

Pre-bake two pricked pie crusts at 400 degrees for 8-15 minutes. Allow to cool. Prepare peach fie filling by combining sugar, water, cornstarch, butter, and salt in a medium saucepan. Cook and stir until thick and clear. Boil 30 seconds or so. Add vanilla and cool slightly. Slice and peel peaches and lightly toss them in mixture. Keep separate from pie crust until serving. Makes 2 large pies. Makes 6-8 servings per pie.

Chocolate Pie

1 gluten-free pie crust, or gluten-free graham cracker crust
1 large + 1 small box chocolate pudding (not instant)
Milk
Whipped topping or whipped cream

Use a 9" pie plate for this amount of pudding. Pre-bake pricked crust at 400 degrees for 8-15 minutes (or prepare graham cracker crust.) Allow to cool. Prepare pudding using the amount of milk specified in instructions on package and pour into cooked pie crust. Allow to set up for several hours. Add whipped topping or whipped cream before serving. Makes 6-8 servings.

Pumpkin Pie

2 gluten-free pie crusts
1 large can of pureed pumpkin
1 ½ c. sugar
½ t. salt
2 t. cinnamon
1 t. ginger
½ t. ground cloves
2 cans evaporated milk, or 2 ½ c. almond or soy milk
4 eggs

Preheat oven to 425 degrees. Place bottom pie crust on pie plate, covering sides and bottom and allowing ½ inch of extra pie crust on outer top edge. Mix pumpkin with remaining ingredients in a large bowl. Pour into uncooked crust. Flute edge of crust. Bake for 15 minutes, and reduce heat to 350 degrees. Bake for 1 hour if using evaporated milk, or until a knife inserted comes out clean. If using almond or soy milk, bake an additional 30-40 minutes. Place aluminum foil on outer edge of crust, if needed, to prevent burning. Makes 6-8 servings per pie.

Carrot Cake

¾ c. garbanzo or fava bean flour
¾ c. rice flour
¼ c. potato flour
¼ c. tapioca flour
2 t. xanthan gum
1 t. baking powder
2 t. baking soda
½ t. salt
1 ½ c. cooking oil
4 eggs
2 c. sugar
2 c. finely grated carrots
1 - 8 oz. can crushed pineapple, drained
Nuts (optional, see directions below)

Preheat oven to 375 degrees. Mix together dry ingredients in large mixing bowl. Beat oil, eggs, sugar, grated carrots, and crushed pineapple for three minutes in another bowl. Add egg mixture to the flour mixture and then add remaining ingredients. Add nuts, if desired. Pour into a greased 9" x 13" pyrex baking pan and bake for 60 to 65 minutes. Cool before frosting with Cream Cheese Frosting (recipe found on next page). Makes 9-12 servings.

Optional:
1 c. chopped pecans or almonds
3 T. honey
2 t. cinnamon
¼ t. nutmeg
1 T. butter

If nuts are desired, place the chopped nuts in small, non-stick, frying pan, and add honey, cinnamon, nutmeg, and butter, and heat until warm.

Cream Cheese Frosting

4 oz. cream cheese, softened
¼ c. butter
1 t. vanilla
½ t. grated lemon peel (optional)
1 ½ c. powdered sugar
1 t. lemon juice

Cream together cream cheese, butter, and vanilla. Add lemon juice, lemon peel (optional), and powdered sugar. Mix until smooth, and frost carrot cake when cool.

Tasty Apple Cake

¾ c. garbanzo or fava bean flour
¾ c. brown rice flour
1 c. sugar
½ t. salt
1 t. baking soda
1 t. baking powder
1 t. cinnamon
½ t. nutmeg
1 t. xanthan gum
2 c. coarsely grated apples
⅓ c. oil
1 beaten egg
1 t. vanilla
½ c. raisins (optional)
1 c. chopped nuts (optional)

Preheat oven to 325 degrees. Combine dry ingredients in large mixing bowl. Combine oil, egg, and vanilla in a small bowl and mix well. Add to the dry ingredients. Add raisins and nuts, if desired. Combine all until mixed. Bake in a 325 degree oven in a greased 8" X 8" baking pan. Bake for approximately 50-60 minutes. Cake will be brown and bounce back if touched in the center. Add caramel sauce and spread over cake. Makes 6-9 servings.

Caramel Sauce

1 cube butter
1 c. brown sugar
4 T. milk

(Continued on next page)

Tasty Apple Cake, Continued

Combine in saucepan and stir while cooking over medium heat until brown sugar is dissolved. Bring to a boil for 1 minute. Pour sauce over hot cake.

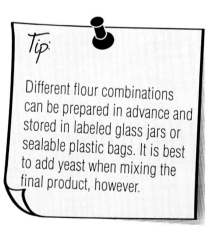

Tip:

Different flour combinations can be prepared in advance and stored in labeled glass jars or sealable plastic bags. It is best to add yeast when mixing the final product, however.

Poppy Seed Cake

3 eggs
1 ⅛ c. canola oil
1 ½ c. milk or soy milk
1 ½ t. almond extract
1 ½ t. butter-flavored extract
1 ½ t. vanilla
2 c. sugar
2 c. rice flour
1 T. corn flour
2 ½ T. sorghum flour
1 ⅛ c. tapioca flour
⅓ c. potato starch
1 t. salt
1 ½ t. baking powder
1 t. xanthan gum
1 T. poppy seeds

Preheat oven to 350 degrees. Blend first 6 ingredients in a mixing bowl. Add dry ingredients and mix until combined. To remove some of the lumps that remain, press the batter with a rubber spatula. Pour batter into greased 9" x 13" baking pan or glass dish. Bake for 40-45 minutes. If a toothpick poked in the center of the cake comes out clean, cake is done. If desired, pour glaze over cake.

For cake, use two 8" or 9" round cake pans. Coat each pan with shortening or cooking spray and line the pan with a cut-out round of waxed paper and spray paper lightly with cooking spray. A 9" X 13" casserole dish can also be used. Bake at 350 degrees for 35-40 minutes or until cake pulls away from sides of the pan, and the center springs back when touched. Makes 9-12 servings.

(Continued on next page)

Poppyseed Cake, Continued

Optional glaze:

¼ c. undiluted limeade or orange juice concentrate
¾ c. powdered sugar
½ t. almond extract
½ t. butter-flavored extract
½ t. vanilla

Bring juice concentrate and powdered sugar to a boil for 1 minute. Remove from heat and add extracts and vanilla. Poke holes in warm cake with a toothpick and drizzle glaze over cake.

Fluffy Frosting

4 c. powdered sugar
¼ c. water
¾ c. shortening
½ t. almond flavoring
½ t. butter flavoring
½ t. vanilla
Pink food coloring (opt.)

Whip ingredients with hand mixer until well mixed.

Cake Decorating Frosting

2 ½ c. powdered sugar
¼ c. shortening
⅛ c. butter, softened
2 t. egg white
¼ t. salt
¼ t. vanilla
¼ t. lemon flavoring
1 t. almond flavoring
2 ½ T. milk

Combine all ingredients and whip for 4-5 minutes on medium speed.

Strawberry Cheesecake

Graham Cracker Crust (see P. 179)
8 oz. cream cheese
1 ½ c. powdered sugar
1 c. whipping cream
1 box strawberry Danish dessert
10-15 strawberries, sliced

Prepare graham cracker crust recipe and press into bottom of 9" X 13" casserole dish. Cream together cream cheese and powdered sugar. Whip cream in a separate bowl. Fold whipped cream into mixture of cream cheese and powdered sugar. Drop by small spoonfuls over crust and spread carefully. Place in fridge. Prepare Danish dessert according to package directions in a saucepan with tall sides. (Mixture splatters as it boils.) Allow to cool slightly while washing and slicing strawberries. Add strawberries to Danish Dessert and mix well. Pour over other layers. Cover cheesecake and allow to set up in fridge for 4-5 hours. Makes 9-12 servings.

Variation of Cheesecake Recipe

Graham Cracker Crust (see P. 179)
2 ½ lbs. cream cheese
1 ¾ c. sugar
3 T. brown rice flour
½ t. grated lemon zest
2 t. vanilla
5 eggs
2 egg yolks
½ c. heavy cream

Press crust into bottom and sides of 9" cheesecake pan and bake. Beat cream cheese in large bowl for 30 seconds. Add sugar, brown rice flour, lemon zest, and vanilla and beat until smooth. Add eggs and egg yolks one at a time and mix. On low speed, add cream. Scoop batter into baked crust and bake at 500 degrees for 12 min., then 200 degrees for 1 hour +. Leave in oven for 30 min. with door ajar. Refrigerate 6 hours.

Angel Food Cake

1 ½ c. powdered sugar
½ c. brown rice flour
¼ c. potato starch
1 t. xanthan gum
¼ c. tapioca flour
1 ½ c. egg whites (about 12 egg whites)
1 ½ t. cream of tartar
1 c. sugar
1 ½ t. vanilla
½ t. almond extract
¼ t. salt
Strawberries
Whipping Cream, with 3 T. powdered sugar added

Heat oven to 375 degrees. Mix powdered sugar (not granulated sugar), rice flour, potato starch, xanthan gum, and tapioca flour in a plastic storage bag or mixing bowl. Set aside. Beat egg whites and cream of tartar in a separate 3-quart bowl on medium speed until foamy. Beat in white sugar on high speed, 1/8 c. at a time, adding vanilla, almond extract, and salt with the last addition of sugar. Continue beating until stiff and glossy. Do not under beat.

Sprinkle powdered sugar-flour mixture, ¼ c. at a time, over meringue, folding in with a rubber spatula until sugar-flour mixture disappears. Spread batter into ungreased angel food cake pan. Cut gently through batter with knife. Bake until cracks on top of cake feel dry and top springs back when touched lightly, about 30-35 minutes. Invert pan on heatproof funnel (or a can of unopened food) until cool. Wash and slice strawberries. Whip the cream and add 3 T. powdered sugar. Combine strawberries and whipped cream. Serve over cake. Makes 6-8 servings.

Brownies

4 eggs, beaten
2 c. sugar
5 T. cocoa
2 t. vanilla
¾ c. rice flour
½ c. tapioca flour
¼ c. potato starch
⅛ c. sorghum flour
⅛ c. corn flour
2 t. xanthan gum
½ lb. melted butter

Preheat oven to 350 degrees. Beat eggs. Add sugar and mix well. Add remaining ingredients, except melted butter and begin mixing. Batter will be thick. Add melted butter gradually. Bake for 35-38 minutes in a greased 9" X 13" baking pan. For a crispier brownie, bake on a greased jelly roll cookie sheet and reduce baking time. Frost with recipe below. Makes 9-12 servings.

Hot Fudge Icing

¼ c. butter
1 c. sugar
¼ c. milk
⅔ c. milk chocolate chips
¾ c. miniature marshmallows
1 t. vanilla

Melt butter in saucepan. Add sugar and milk. Boil for one minute. Take off the heat and add chocolate chips, marshmallows and vanilla. Stir until well mixed. Let the frosting cool before spreading on brownies or frosting will be runny.

White Grape Juice Delight

1 can frozen white grape juice concentrate
Water
1 ½ c. lemon-lime soda, chilled

In a large pitcher, prepare white grape juice by adding water according to directions on can. Add soda. Mix well.

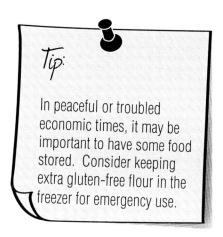

Tip:

In peaceful or troubled economic times, it may be important to have some food stored. Consider keeping extra gluten-free flour in the freezer for emergency use.

Icy Lemonade

1 can frozen lemonade concentrate
30 ice cubes
4 c. lemon-lime soda, chilled

Prepare recipe in blender by adding half of the ingredients at a time. Blend until ice is crushed. Repeat.

Tip:

Gluten-free noodles, spaghetti sauce, rice, potato flakes, canned chicken, water, powdered milk, canned fruits, and canned vegetables are all possible foods to have for emergencies.

Homemade Root Beer

5 lbs. sugar
5 gallons water
1 bottle root beer concentrate
5 lb. block of dry ice

Combine first three ingredients in large 10 gallon insulated drink cooler container. Using clean gloves, add dry ice to mixture.

Tip:

When using emergency food storage, substitute canned chicken in place of fresh chicken in selected recipes that your family enjoys.

Grape Juice Lemonade

12 oz. can frozen grape juice concentrate
12 oz. can frozen lemonade concentrate
3 cans lemon-lime soda
½ c. sugar

In large insulated drink cooler container, prepare grape juice and lemonade and mix them together. Add soda and soda and mix well.

Tip:

Natural disasters are becoming more common. An emergency kit with a 72 hour supply of gluten-free food is a good idea.

Orange Juice Refresher

6 oz. frozen orange juice concentrate
2 c. milk
½ c. sugar
1 t. vanilla
¼ c. powdered vanilla drink mix
12 ice cubes

Combine all in blender until smooth.

Tip:

For a delicious variation, replace the orange juice with other juices, such as white grape juice, raspberry lemonade, fruit medley, etc.

Delicious Slush

1 can strawberry guava juice concentrate
1 liter bottle of Fresca®

Prepare juice in a large pitcher by adding water according to instructions on can. Freeze juice. Pour soda over juice. As it softens, break up frozen juice. Pour mixture into large punch bowl for serving, if desired.

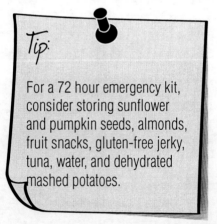

Tip:

For a 72 hour emergency kit, consider storing sunflower and pumpkin seeds, almonds, fruit snacks, gluten-free jerky, tuna, water, and dehydrated mashed potatoes.

Hot Chocolate Mix

This recipe is large and is great to share at Christmas time.

2 lb. container chocolate drink mix
1 box dried milk (to make 8 quarts)
1 - 16 oz. container non-dairy creamer
1 c. powdered sugar

Combine well and serve by adding 3 T. to 1 c. of warm milk.

Tip:

Surprise your family and tell them you are pretending there is an emergency. Take your 72 hour kit to a nearby park and test it out. Rotate food that may have expired.

Carol, age 79

In 1967, after the birth of my eighth child, I had a break-down in my health, which included osteoarthritis. In 1996, I was diagnosed with celiac sprue. The diagnosis did not come about because I exhibited textbook symptoms of celiac. I was essentially asymptomatic. It was discovered because my rheumatologist asked me to participate in a drug study for a new medicine that was being developed for arthritis.

In order to be eligible for the study I had to have a endoscopy to determine that my stomach lining had not been damaged by NSAIDS. I had no problems with the stomach lining, but this laboratory procedure showed that I had GERD, esophagitis, short Barrett's esophagus (a pre-cursor of cancer), and celiac sprue.

When the doctor told his partners that he had found a case of celiac sprue, they questioned his diagnosis. The pictures that he took were very definitive, however, as was the blood test that followed. His partners have become believers and encourage their patients to come to our support group meetings for people with celiac disease. All of my doctors have since expressed their opinion that the undiagnosed celiac was the underlying cause of my three bone diseases, compressed discs, and digestive diseases.

So far six of my children and several grandchildren have tested positive and have had improved health since following the gluten-free diet. I am encouraged that in the years since my diagnosis, the medical profession has become increasingly aware of celiac disease, especially when there are health problems with seemingly no underlying cause.

Meal Planning and Misc.

Meal Planning

Main Dish Menu Ideas

Week 1

1. Baked Whole Chicken
2. Beef Stroganoff
3. Sweet and Sour Meatballs
4. Fried Fish and Irish Nachos
5. Tacos and Chili Relleno Casserole
6. Shrimp Stir Fry
7. Easy Vegetable Noodle Casserole

Week 2

1. Roast Beef
2. Chinese Noodles
3. Baked Potato Bar
4. Chinese Sweet and Sour
5. Seasoned Pork Chops
6. Parmesan Cheese Chicken
7. Chicken Fettuccine

Week 3

1. Steak
2. Taco Salad and Quick Chicken Tortillas
3. Creamy Chicken Enchiladas
4. Hawaiian Haystacks
5. Bacon Ranch Hamburgers
6. Alfredo Pizza
7. Honey Mustard Chicken

Meal Planning, Cont'd.

Week 4

1. Steak Fajitas
2. Pineapple Chicken Lo Mien
3. Meatloaf
4. Spaghetti
5. BBQ Pork Chops
6. Hot and Spicy Chicken
7. Paprika Chicken

Week 5

1. Lemon Chicken
2. Shepherd's Pie
3. Grilled Salmon
4. Beef Enchiladas
5. Pizza
6. Thai Red Curry
7. Sweet and Sour Pork

Week 6

1. Sweet Pear Pork Chops
2. Japanese Style Chicken
3. Red Sauce Creamy Enchiladas
4. Pork Roast
5. Green Chili Tacos
6. BBQ Chicken
7. Chili Potato Topping

Meal Planning, Cont'd.

Week 7

1. Chili
2. Sweet and Sour Chicken
3. Chicken Strips
4. Salt and Vinegar Chicken
5. Slow Cooked Roast
6. Tortilla Wrap Idea (see Main Dish section)
7. Chicken with Sweet Lemon Sauce

Week 8

1. Lasagna
2. BBQ Meatballs
3. Tortilla Wrap Idea (see Main Dish section)
4. Chicken Fajitas (see recipe for Steak Fajitas)
5. Italian Chicken
6. Mexican Sausage Bake or Omelets
7. Honey Garlic Chicken

Cold Weather Soups ❄

(substitute in place of another menu item when desired)

1. Clam Chowder
2. Thai Noodle Soup
3. Enchilada Soup
4. Baked Potato Soup
5. Chicken Taco Soup
6. Turkey Burger Soup
7. Minestrone Soup
8. Potato Bean Soup
9. Sausage Kale Soup
10. Cream of Broccoli Soup
11. Fiesta Soup
12. Chicken/Turkey Noodle Soup
13. Beef Taco Soup
14. Curried Chicken Rice Soup
15. Cream of Rice Soup
16. Potato Cheese Soup

Peanut Butter Play Dough

1 c. creamy peanut butter
1 ¼ c. dry milk
1 c. light corn syrup
1 ¼ c. powdered sugar

Pour all ingredients into a sealed bag. Knead until dough forms.

Rice Flour Play Dough

2 ¼ c. rice flour
1 ¾ c. salt
1 T. cream of tartar
2 ½ T. canola oil
2 c. colored water

Heat over medium heat until thickened, remove from heat, and then knead. If playdough is too sticky, add more rice flour.

Toasted Pumpkin Seeds

1 c. pumpkin seeds
1 T. canola oil or melted butter
Salt

Preheat oven to 350 degrees. Wash pumpkin seeds and dry them on a paper towel. Place pumpkin seeds in a plastic bag or bowl. Mix seeds with canola oil or melted butter. Spread seeds on baking sheet and sprinkle with salt. Bake for 15-20 minutes, stirring several times.

Canning Recipes

*All canning recipes are subject to change according to the latest methods of home canning. Please check the instruction manual that comes with your canner.

Grape Juice

Concord grapes
½ c. sugar per quart jar
Boiling water

Fill clean sink around half full with cold water and add Concord grapes. Remove good grapes from stems and rinse under cold water. Fill quart jar about ½ full with grapes. Add ½ c. sugar, and fill to ½" head space with boiling water. Simmer lids and allow to stay in hot water for at least 3-4 minutes. Add lids and canning rings and tighten. Place the filled jars in the canner and cover completely with water. Turn heat to high and begin timing when the water is boiling. Turn heat down to medium high and process 15 minutes in boiling water bath. Check to be sure that a softly rolling boil is maintained. Drain grape juice from grapes when serving. Wait until sugar dissolves in the bottom of the jars before using grape juice.

Canning Recipes, Cont'd.

Peaches

Ripened peaches
½ c. sugar per quart
Boiling water

Blanche peaches by submerging them in boiling water for about 15 seconds. Place them in a clean sink filled around halfway full with cold water. Cut peach in half and remove skin and pit. Wash well and fill quart jar, allowing 1" space at top of jar. Pour ½ c. sugar over fruit in jar. Add boiling water to ½" head space. Simmer lids and allow to stay in hot water for at least 3-4 minutes. Add lids and canning rings and tighten. Place the filled jars in the canner and cover completely with water. Turn heat to high and begin timing when the water is boiling. Check to be sure that a softly rolling boil is maintained. Turn heat down to medium high and process 20 minutes in boiling water bath.

Canning Recipes, Cont'd.

Raspberries

Raspberries
2 c. sugar
5 c. water

Wash 5-6 pint jars. Fill clean sink and add raspberries. Let them soak for several minutes and lightly rinse them under a gentle stream of water. Try not to handle them too much. Fill pints ⅔ full with raspberries. Bring water and sugar to a boil until sugar dissolves. Fill to ½" head space with water/sugar solution. Simmer lids and allow to stay in hot water for at least 3-4 minutes. Add lids and canning rings and tighten. Place the filled jars in the canner and cover completely with water. Turn heat to high and begin timing when the water is boiling. Check to be sure that a softly rolling boil is maintained. Turn heat down to medium high and process 10 minutes in boiling water bath.

Canning Recipes, Cont'd.

Apple Pie Filling

12 quarts sliced McIntosh apples
5 quarts water
5 c. sugar
1 t. nutmeg
1 c. cornstarch
1 T. cinnamon
1 t. salt
2 T. lemon juice

Wash 8 quart jars. Slice, core, peel, and wash apples. Place in large pot with water. Cook for 10 minutes to shrink apples. Remove apples by using slotted spoon. Add remaining ingredients to juice from apples. Cook until thickened and add apples. Fill the quart jars to ½" head space. Simmer lids and allow to stay in hot water for at least 3-4 minutes. Place lids and canning rings on jars and tighten. Place the filled jars in the canner and cover completely with water. Turn heat to high and begin timing when the water is boiling. Check to be sure that a softly rolling boil is maintained. Turn heat down to medium high and process 20 minutes in boiling water bath.

Canning Recipes, Cont'd.

Pears

Ripened pears
½ c. sugar per quart
Boiling water

Use carrot peeler to remove skin from pears. Cut pear in half and remove seeds with small metal measuring spoon. Wash pears well and fill quart jar, allowing 1" space at top of jar. Pour ½ c. sugar over fruit in jar. Add boiling water. Simmer lids and allow to stay in hot water for at least 3-4 minutes. Add lids and canning rings and tighten. Place the filled jars in the canner and cover completely with water. Turn heat to high and begin timing when the water is boiling. Check to be sure that a softly rolling boil is maintained. Turn heat down to medium high and process 20 minutes in boiling water bath.

Canning Recipes, Cont'd.

Applesauce

1 lb. apples (An average of 19 pounds is needed per canner load of 7 quarts or 12 to 14 pounds for 9 pints.)
¼ c. sugar
⅛ t. salt

Wash, cut apples into quarters, peel, and core. Place in heavy 8 to 10 quart pan for a canner batch of applesauce. Add ¾ cup of water (if using 19 lbs. apples) and heat the apples over medium heat, stirring often to move apple slices from bottom to top. Heat until apples are tender. Pour apples into a food strainer/sauce maker. Pour hot applesauce into clean jars to ½" head space. Simmer lids and allow to stay in hot water for at least 3-4 minutes. Add lids and canning rings and tighten. Place the filled jars in the canner and cover completely with water. Turn heat to high and begin timing when the water is boiling. Check to be sure that a softly rolling boil is maintained. Turn heat down to medium high and process 20 minutes in boiling water bath.

Canning Recipes, Cont'd.

Dill Pickles

Cucumbers to fill 7 jars
12 c. water
6 c. apple cider vinegar
¾ c. salt
7 heads of fresh dill
14 cloves garlic

Wash 7 quart jars. Wash cucumbers and soak in ice water for 24 hours. Drain cucumbers. Place 1 head of dill and 2 garlic cloves in the bottom of each quart jar. Boil water, vinegar, and salt for one minute. (Less brine may be needed, depending on whether slices or whole pickles are desired.) Place cucumbers in jars. Pour water, vinegar, and salt mixture over cucumbers and fill the quart jars to ½" head space. Simmer lids and allow to stay in hot water for at least 3-4 minutes. Add lids and canning rings and tighten. Bring water to a boil in canner. Add quarts of pickles to boiling water using a bottle lifter. Use caution to avoid getting burned by the boiling water. Process in boiling water bath for 15 minutes. Wait 2-3 weeks before eating pickles.

Canning Recipes, Cont'd.

Dill Beans

Green beans, with ends removed
1 clove garlic per jar
1 sprig dill weed per jar
¼ t. alum per jar
Mrs. Wages Dill Pickle Mix (see pkg. instructions)
  or the following brine:
 2 c. water
1 c. white vinegar
2 T. noniodized salt

In each pint jar, place one clove garlic, a sprig of dill weed, and ¼ t. alum. Line with beans. Bring brine to a boil and pour over beans to ½" head space. Simmer lids and allow to stay in hot water for at least 3-4 minutes. Add lids and canning rings and tighten. Place the filled jars in the canner and cover completely with water. Turn heat to high and begin timing when the water is boiling. Check to be sure that a softly rolling boil is maintained. Turn heat down to medium high and process 7 minutes in boiling water bath.

Canning Recipes, Cont'd.

Tomato Juice

6 quarts tomatoes
2 c. onions (in quarters)
2 c. celery
6 bay leaves
Salt, to taste

Wash 5 quart jars. Cook ingredients together until tender. Remove bay leaves. Pour mixture through food mill. Add salt, to taste. Fill the quart jars to ½" head space with tomato juice. Simmer lids and allow to stay in hot water for at least 3-4 minutes. Add lids and canning rings and tighten. Place the filled jars in the canner and cover completely with water. Turn heat to high and begin timing when the water is boiling. Check to be sure that a softly rolling boil is maintained. Turn heat down to medium high and process 10 minutes in boiling water bath.

Canning Recipes, Cont'd.

Frozen Corn

30 c. corn (cut from cob)
12 c. water
1 c. sugar
¼ c. salt

Place each cob of corn on hole of angel food cake pan. Using an electric knife, carefully slice corn off of cob into cake pan, rotating cob as you go. Measure corn and combine with water, sugar, and salt in very large pot or canner. Simmer for 20 minutes. When cool enough, place in fridge. Or add a block of ice or ice cubes within a clean bag to hot corn to cool it quickly. Place corn in plastic sealable freezer bags and freeze.

Canning Recipes, Cont'd.

*Due to the dangers of using a pressure canner, do not use this recipe without a thorough reading of the process of pressure canning. Use the manual that came with your pressure canner. The boiling water bath method is not allowable for beans.

Green Beans

Green beans
1 t. salt per quart
Boiling water

Remove ends of beans. Snap and wash beans. Put 1 t. salt in a quart jar. Fill quart jar with green beans, allowing 1" space at top of jar. Add boiling water to ½" head space. Simmer lids and allow to stay in hot water for at least 3-4 minutes. Add lids and canning rings and tighten. Place jars in pressure canner with 2 quarts of hot water (check pressure canner instructions to verify water amount). Lock pressure canner lid. Turn heat on high and when pressure builds in canner (approximately 15-20 min.) to 15 lbs. pressure (for quarts), begin timing. It is important to check canner pressure often to make sure it is staying at 15 lbs. pressure. Turn heat down to medium high and process for 25 minutes. Process 20 minutes for pints. Certain types of pressure canners can be tested by a hardware store or county agent to ensure the pressure reading is correct.

Canning Recipes, Cont'd.

Salsa

5 quarts tomatoes, peeled and quartered
3 bell peppers, red or green
3 yellow bell peppers
2 ½ jalapeno peppers (remove some seeds for milder salsa)
2 Anahiem peppers (long, green type)
2 long red peppers
2 large onions, diced
3 cloves garlic, minced

Peel and quarter tomatoes. Dice all peppers and add to the tomatoes. Add onions and garlic. Cook all in large pot until tender (about 1 hour). Stir occasionally. Then add:

1 ½ t. paprika
⅓ c. sugar
½ c. apple cider vinegar
1 ½ t. coarse ground pepper
¼ c. canning salt
1 ½ t. cumin
1 ½ t. garlic salt
½ bunch of cilanto
1 quart tomato paste (optional)

Simmer for 1 hour. Stir occasionally. Wash quarts or pints. Fill the jars to ½" head space. Simmer lids and allow to stay in hot water for at least 3-4 minutes. Add lids and canning rings and tighten. Place the filled jars in the canner and cover completely with water. Turn heat to high and begin timing when the water is boiling. Check to be sure that a softly rolling boil is maintained. Turn heat down to medium high and process 25 minutes in boiling water bath. Makes 8-14 pints or 4-7 quarts.

Lessons Learned

*This information is subject to change. Please understand the necessity of reading labels for the latest information.

Some dried fruit may be coated with wheat flour to prevent it from sticking together. Banana chips are often coated with flour.

Medicine and vitamins may contain gluten. A website to check might be glutenfreedrugs.com.

Deli roast beef (and other types of lunch meat) can contain wheat in the broth used to moisten the meat.

Some prepared, flavored rice in packets (or served in restaurants) may contain wheat.

Even though allergen statements may list that the product doesn't have wheat, it may contain gluten in the form of barley (malt), rye, or cross-contaminated oats. An example might be a candy bar containing crispy rice.

Several people in our local support group have felt there was a connection between the irritation to the skin/scalp and the wheat in their lotion/hair products.

When eating at restaurants, it is important that the employees understand the concept of cross-contamination on grills and in cooking oil. French fries cooked in the same oil as chicken nuggets would not be considered gluten-free. Many restaurants have gluten-free menus that are available online.

Breath mints may contain wheat maltodextrin. Gum may also contain wheat, as well as coated nuts.

Lessons Learned, Cont'd.

Lipstick may contain wheat.

Some potato chips now have wheat flour or wheat maltodextrin in them. Maltodextrin, listed by itself, does not contain wheat or barley. It would seem that maltodextrin would contain barley because of the word "malt" in the word "maltodextrin." However, this is not the case.

Make sure you have your own peanut butter, jam, jelly, butter, honey, mayonnaise, etc.. Labeling will help prevent cross-contamination.

Corn tortillas and tostadas may have cross-contamination from flour tortillas in the same facility. Check the label. Wheat flour is used in the production of some corn tortillas to make the tortillas more firm. A fast food establishment or restaurant should be able to refer to the labels on the boxes in which the tortillas were shipped and help you with this needed information.

Be certain to read the label for these products: frosting, beef broth/bouillon, seasoning mix, gravy mix, hot dogs, salami, flavored tortilla chips, trail mix, artificial crab, marinades, and soy sauce.

Purchased play dough often has wheat. For young children who tend to lick their fingers, it may be important to make homemade playdough (see Meal Planning/Misc. section).

Buy an extra toaster to be used for gluten-free bread. Label it, "For gluten-free bread only". Toaster ovens can also be used and the oven rack can be washed thoroughly.

Lessons Learned, Cont'd.

Be aware that some people are so sensitive that touching gluten products or being exposed to breathing the white or wheat flour dust can affect them.

Modified food starch produced in the USA is commonly made from corn. Also, caramel color, artificial flavors, and artificial colors are all usually gluten-free in this country.

When children who have celiac disease have gone to an event where they have been deprived of a treat, it may be helpful to have a supply of gluten-free candy at home to give them when they arrive home. If possible, send the treat with them to the event.

Serving gluten-free pizza from the health food store (or homemade) can help ease the disappointment felt from missing out on pizza with gluten.

The diagnosis of this disease is still variable and difficult for most of the medical profession. Most of the people in our support group have been ill and have consulted numerous doctors before discovering that they have gluten intolerance.

The huge range of symptoms contributes to the difficulties of diagnosis.

Read labels! Companies are usually very helpful and many phone numbers are toll free. If you have a question about the product, call the company to verify that there is no gluten.

There are many great foods to eat! With practice, a wonderful gluten-free lifestyle can be established.

Index by Name

Index by Category

A

B

F

G

H